Advance praise for *Can You Say a Few Words?*

"Let me say a few words about Joan Detz: Her books are great."

> —Roger Ailes, top presidential and
> corporate communications consultant,
> and author of
> *You Are the Message*

"*Can You Say a Few Words?* by Joan Detz has helped me to speak better. I recommend this book to anyone who wishes to use words well."

> —Norman Vincent Peale, author of
> *The Power of Positive Thinking*

"Joan Detz's book *Can You Say a Few Words?* is imaginative, practical and necessary. All of us who are asked to speak can learn a great deal from it. Keep it close by."

> —Stephen D. Harlan, Vice Chairman,
> KPMG Peat Marwick

"If you are a leader in business or the community, this concise manual belongs on your desk next to the dictionary. Joan Detz is the Emily Post of speech communication. She tells you what's right, what's wrong, what works, what doesn't work. You don't have to wing it anymore."

> —James F. Fox, past president,
> Public Relations Society of America

CAN YOU SAY
A FEW WORDS?

Also by Joan Detz
  How to Write & Give a Speech
  You Mean I Have to Stand Up and Say Something?

CAN YOU SAY
A FEW WORDS?

Joan Detz

ST. MARTIN'S GRIFFIN ❧ NEW YORK

Design by Dawn Niles

www.stmartins.com

Library of Congress Cataloging-in-Publication Data

Detz, Joan.
    Can you say a few words / Joan Detz.
        p. cm.
    ISBN 0-312-06014-9 (hc)
    ISBN 0-312-05830-6 (pbk)
    1. Public speaking. I. Title.
    PN4121.D3877   1991
    808.5'1—dc20   90-28421
                                                        CIP

First St. Martin's Griffin Edition: June 1991

D 10 9 8 7 6 5

CONTENTS

ACKNOWLEDGMENTS

This is the second time I've been able to work on a book with Barbara Anderson as my editor, and I count myself very fortunate. Barbara is a terrific editor. She takes pride in her books, and she works hard on her authors' behalf. I've benefited from her advice, and I'm enormously grateful.

I would like to thank the reference librarians at both the Brooklyn Business Library and the New York Public Library. Their expertise saved me countless hours.

My special appreciation goes to the librarians at the main branch of the Bucks County Free Library in Doylestown, Pennsylvania. These wonderful people answered question after question—accurately, quickly, and with amazing patience. I have always admired librarians in general; I have the highest admiration for these librarians in particular.

I would like to acknowledge my gratitude to Jim Fox, my speechwriting mentor. Years ago, I attended the speechwriting workshop Jim taught for New York University. I wrote a pretty good speech when I went into Jim's class; I wrote a far better one when I came out. Speechwriters all across this country are indebted to Jim Fox for the sound speechwriting instruction he's given over the years. I'm pleased to use this space to offer the public thank-you he deserves.

Above all, I would like to thank my husband, Ira Rubinstein. His editorial judgment, his common sense, and his unwavering support made all the difference.

INTRODUCTION

It usually starts out simply enough:

- Your manager drops by the office and says, "I'm holding a special staff meeting this afternoon. Can you just say a few words about the new project?"

- Your alma mater calls and asks you to say a few words at the annual alumni dinner.

- A senior executive dies, and you're expected to say a few words at the memorial service.

- Your company wants to give you a service award, and you'll have to say a few words at the ceremony.

- Your team wins the state championship, and your principal asks you to say a few words at the victory banquet.

- Your parents celebrate their 50th anniversary, and you'll want to say a few words at their party.

- Your child's teacher says, "We want to raise money for the school library. Can you say a few words to launch our fund-raising drive?"

Well, that's the big question: *Can* you?

Can you "say a few words" that will capture the audience's attention, keep their interest, and further your cause? What's more, can you prepare under deadline pressure?

All too often, the answer is no.

The sad truth is, most people would rather do *anything* than stand

1

up and say a few words. And the emotional stress that often goes hand in hand with these special occasions makes your job even harder.

I know. For more than a decade, I've been writing speeches for top executives across America. And I've seen accomplished speakers turn to mush when they had to make an emotional retirement speech. I've seen confident administrators lose control when they had to offer a eulogy. I've seen tough CEOs grin like kids and stammer with embarrassment when they had to accept an award.

Special occasions *demand* special speeches. And sorry is the speaker who doesn't live up to the audience's demands.

One man, a highly competent executive, told me, "It's funny. I've faced angry shareholders; I've given lots of financial presentations. But when I had to pay a farewell tribute to a colleague . . . well, that was the toughest speaking assignment I ever got. I wanted to come up with something really special to suit the occasion, but I just didn't know where to begin."

And he's not alone. I've heard similar stories from speakers in all walks of life.

I lecture on speechwriting throughout the country—to *Fortune* 500 corporations, professional organizations, colleges, all sorts of groups. Invariably, someone in my seminar will say, "I've got a problem. I have to introduce my boss at a big conference, and I don't know how to start. What makes a good introduction? Can you give me some pointers?"

Yes, I can. And that's exactly what I'm going to do in this book.

I've written my book in three sections. Part 1 is organized alphabetically by occasion. So if you're in a hurry—and who isn't?—you can turn straight to the relevant chapter: awards, building dedications, eulogies, prayers, retirement tributes, toasts, whatever.

You'll get quick advice, podium-tested examples, and practical tips that will help you "say a few words" for *any* special occasion.

Part 2's chapter is called "Do You Feel a Little Nervous?" If you're worried about podium jitters . . . well, worry no more. Turn to Part 2 and get real-life tips that can help you control your nervousness.

Part 3 offers dozens of examples that can give your speeches more style. If you want to create speeches that are more lively, more interesting, and more memorable, turn to this section and see how the top speakers do it.

And at the end you'll find an appendix that describes lots of useful reference books where you can find terrific quotations and anecdotes.

The advice in this book has proven helpful to my clients over the years. I hope it proves helpful to you—so the next time someone asks you to "say a few words," you'll be able to give a speech that's as special as the occasion.

The best of luck!

PART 1

SPECIAL OCCASIONS

ANNIVERSARIES

Life is all memory except for the one present moment that goes
by so quickly you can hardly catch it going.

—TENNESSEE WILLIAMS

Your principal completes 20 years of service, and the teachers want
to host an anniversary party. Your company celebrates 100 years in business. Your department store wants to salute employees who've completed
10 years on the job.

How can you come up with a speech that's as special as the occasion? Here are nine ideas for an anniversary speech people will remember
long after the event is over:

1. Turn Back the Clock

People love to reminisce, to go back into history, to remember the
way things used to be. So turn back the clock 20 years, 100 years, 10
years—whatever.

What were the hit songs, the hit movies, the hit TV shows? What
news made front page headlines? Who won the World Series?

In short, what were people talking about when this principal or
this company or this employee got started? Use those details to grab the
audience's attention.

For example, you could say, "Back in 1974, people were humming
'You and Me Against the World,' and standing in line to see *The Godfa-
ther, Part II,* and doing anything to get tickets for a new Broadway show
called *A Chorus Line.*

"Hank Aaron broke Babe Ruth's lifetime home run record, the
House Judiciary Committee recommended impeachment of Richard
Nixon, and Muhammad Ali regained his heavyweight boxing champi-
onship.

7

"And, here at Penn High School, a new principal by the name of Jim Smith came on board. Today, 20 years later, we're all gathered to salute his talents, his dedication, and his achievements."

2. Honor the Founder or Owner

Ask yourself, who's the person behind this success story?

For the 50th anniversary of Carlson Companies, an intimate little crowd of 4,000 employees, customers, suppliers, and public officials attended a celebration dinner in St. Paul, Minnesota—with none other than Bob Hope serving as the master of ceremonies.

Hope dubbed the owner of the $4.2 billion Carlson empire "Super Swede." Hope even performed his own theme song, "Thanks for the Memories," with a special twist to honor Mr. Carlson:

> Thanks for the firm you built
> In '38 you planted the seed
> And it has grown indeed
> You started out small
> Now you own it all
> Even the king calls you Super Swede.
> How lucky you were.

3. Recognize Changes That Have Occurred Over the Years

Have the passing years brought big changes, big improvements? If so, point them out.

When Grant Dove, CEO of Microelectronic and Computer Technology, spoke at his organization's fifth anniversary in Austin, Texas, he pointed out these changes since the company was started:

> It's been five years since MCC opened its doors here in Austin, marking the first time U.S. industry joined together to under-

8

take cooperative long-term research in microelectronics and computer technology. . . .

Where there was once just a vision of cooperative research, we now have five major research programs.

Where there was once just a hope for collaboration among companies, we now have companies coming together to create value!

4. Cite the Good Qualities That Have Remained Constant Over the Years

Has the person kept a sense of courage, of curiosity, of fairness? Has the company honored its founding principles—even during tough times? Has the organization remained true to its original goals?

If so, cite these qualities, and remind the audience of their current value.

5. Urge People to Keep Their Tradition of Excellence

When James Renier, CEO of Honeywell Incorporated, spoke to the Omicron Delta Kappa National Convention, he said:

> I congratulate you on your 75th anniversary. Somebody once asked Abbott Lawrence Lowell, president of Harvard, what it takes to make a great university. His answer was, "300 years."
>
> Well, 300 years is reasonable if you're talking about Harvard. But most organizations have to make their mark more quickly. And some, like Omicron Delta Kappa, are able to do a great deal in a short time. . . .
>
> Wherever you have gone, you have taught and encouraged leadership. I hope you will keep that objective. It seems the demand for leadership always exceeds the supply.

6. State Your Beliefs

Anniversaries are a good time to restate your philosophy.

When Lyndon Johnson marked the 10th anniversary of the Government Employees Incentive Awards Act at a ceremony at Constitution Hall in Philadelphia, he said, "I believe in the tight fist and the open mind—a tight fist with money and an open mind to the needs of America."

7. Use an Inspirational Quotation or a Bit of Local Color

When the University of Pennsylvania celebrated its 250th anniversary, President Sheldon Hackney tapped into the university's origins as a "charity school" established by Ben Franklin.

Quoting an inspirational line from a 1749 Franklin pamphlet, President Hackney said, "The great aim and end of all learning is to be able to serve others. That is why our university exists. That is why all universities should exist."

8. Share Your Joy

Celebrating a big wedding anniversary? Now's a good time to talk about the joy you've known throughout these years.

When Jennie and Todd Eppley, of Marysville, Pennsylvania, celebrated their 50th wedding anniversary, Jennie spoke of the joy she had received from her own parents, from her son, and from her husband. And, she concluded with three little words that applied to *everyone* at the celebration: "I love you."

9. Say It With Something Other Than Words

Don't feel you have to rely on words alone. Anniversary celebrations can be enriched by:

- *Silence* When world leaders gathered to honor the 75th anniversary of the battle of Gallipoli, Australian and British warships fired their guns, and everyone observed one minute of silence.

- *Applause* When a popular retiree returned to a company's anniversary event, no words seemed adequate to express the goodwill in the air. So the audience simply rose and applauded with great enthusiasm.

- *Song* When a coach celebrated his fifth winning season, his team honored him with a rousing rendition of the school song.

AWARDS: GIVING THEM AND GETTING THEM

Did one of your employees submit a prize-winning suggestion? Did a member of your speakers bureau earn a service citation? Did a teacher on your staff get national recognition?

When you present an award on these special occasions, you'll want to give a speech that's equally special—a speech filled with praise, admiration, and respect for the honoree.

Of course, you'll also want to give a speech when you're the recipient of an award—an acceptance speech filled with gratitude, appreciation, and respect for the group that's honoring you.

GIVING AN AWARD

Dost thou wish to be applauded? Applaud another.

—SAINT JOHN CHRYSOSTOM, C. A.D 388

Here are seven ideas that can help you give an award speech that's more personal, more inspirational, and more memorable:

1. Talk About How You Know the Honoree

Have you worked on the same programs? Did you join the company at the same time? Do you live in the same neighborhood, go to the same church, or do volunteer work for the same causes?

If so, make that connection clear to the audience. They'll appreciate the personal ties.

A caution: if you *don't* know the person who's getting the award, don't pretend. Audiences are quick to spot a phony connection.

12

Instead, say something simple and sincere: "I've heard many fine things about Paul, and I'm pleased to meet him tonight. The plant foreman told me about Paul's heroic efforts, and it's a joy to present him with our company's humanitarian award."

2. Cite the High Caliber of Previous Recipients

Here's how C. J. Silas, CEO of Phillips Petroleum Company, opened an award speech:

> Thank you . . . for inviting me to take part in the induction of four outstanding leaders into the Alabama Business Hall of Fame. Tom Moore tells me that when the board of visitors organized the hall of fame in 1973, it was the first of its kind in the nation.
> Since then, you've been the standard by which other such halls of fame have sprung up nationwide.
> In the process, you've honored dozens of Alabama business leaders—not just for their accomplishments, but for their character.

3. Paint the Big Picture

Let's suppose you're honoring an employee for a suggestion that will save the company x dollars each year. Why not multiply that figure by the total number of employees to show the great potential of these money-saving suggestions?

4. Praise Sacrifice

Did your recipient drive through a blizzard to meet her obligations? Work on weekends to complete his project? Postpone her vacation to provide a crucial service?

Cite that sacrifice. Offer generous praise. Extraordinary contributions deserve extraordinary award speeches.

5. Create a Sense of Urgency

When I conduct speechwriting workshops, I'm often asked for ways to "spice up" an award ceremony. As one workshop participant put it, "Since our utility hands out service awards every year, the program gets stale after a while."

You can make an award ceremony seem fresh by giving it a sense of immediacy.

Here's how Louis Cabot, chairman of the board of directors of the Brookings Institute, created a sense of urgency at a presentation of the Benjamin Rush Award at Dickinson College:

> My subject may sound at first like old hat—the importance of science in a liberal arts education. It is an old subject, but one I feel strongly about. . . .
>
> My purpose is to erase any complacency you have about science in your lives and to replace it with a sense of urgency and alarm. . . .
>
> I believe man will do more to shake up the human race in your generation and the next 10 generations than in all the 100,000 generations of man that have gone before us. And, we are not prepared for it.

6. Use Interesting Statistics

Statistics don't have to be boring. Listen to the vivid statistics that Dr. David Snediker, vice president of Battelle, used when he spoke at an awards reception in Ohio:

> In 1965, a mechanic could fix any car on the road if he or she understood 5,000 pages of service manuals. But today, that mechanic has to be able to comprehend 465,000 pages. That's the equivalent of 250 Columbus telephone books!

7. Cite Qualities That Make the Recipient Uniquely Valued

Be specific. Give real-life examples. Tell a flattering anecdote about the person. Show what makes this person special.

A warning: Speakers who make demeaning or bigoted comments about a person's race, religion, age, sex, or ethnic background do not deserve an audience's respect. I once heard a manager make the unfortunate comment, "This is the first time I've ever had a Hispanic person I could give an award to."

And I once watched a senior executive botch an award ceremony by the way he presented the service pins. First he placed a pin on the lapel of the male recipient. Then he approached the female recipient, hesitated, turned to the audience and said, "Back in the old days, when we didn't hire women managers, you didn't have to worry about how to put a pin on a woman's chest." He thrust the pin into the poor woman's hand and left her looking totally embarrassed.

Think and plan ahead about what you will say *and do,* to avoid such gaffes.

GETTING AN AWARD

> Publishers and literary agents once told me I could never make a success at writing about Chinese people. I thought of that the day I stood before the King of Sweden to receive the Nobel Prize.
>
> —PEARL S BUCK

Accepting an award is a great honor—exciting, prestigious, and touching. But it can also be a little bit scary. Scary because the audience has such high expectations. How can you ever meet them?

Well, you could always follow in the footsteps of Yogi Berra, who once began an acceptance speech by saying, "I want to thank all the people who made this night necessary."

But if that's not your style, maybe you'll find some inspiration in the following approaches:

Express Affection for the Organization

When Jimmy Stewart was honored by the Film Society of Lincoln Center in New York City, he responded with great affection: "I ask God to bless all of you, and when he takes our lives to his editing room, I pray he will be as kind to each of you as you've been to me tonight."

Share Your Award With Those Who Deserve Credit

Listen to the beautiful power of this acceptance speech by Cynthia Ann Broad, a special-education teacher who was named Michigan Teacher of the Year. Try reading the excerpt aloud so you can appreciate the full impact of her message:

16

. . . Truly, it is my students who won this award for me.

I discussed the nominating questions for this award with my students. I said I had a problem.

They asked, "What's your problem?"

I answered, "One of the questions asks me what makes an outstanding teacher. I'm not sure if I *am* an outstanding teacher, even if that's what I try to be."

One of my students replied, "If this award was for *us,* would you have a problem?"

I immediately answered, "No!"

And they said, "Well, get this award for us—our room could sure use this big award."

So, to my students, I'd like to say thank you for helping me, and working with me, to solve our problems together. Thank you for helping me become Michigan's Teacher of the Year.

Acknowledge the Support of Your Family

If your family has been a source of inspiration, say so.

When singer Tracy Chapman received a Grammy Award, she expressed these personal thank-yous: "To my mother, who bought me my first guitar, and to my sister, who is my best critic, my best audience, and my best friend."

Express Your Humility

When Billy Graham was offered a star on Hollywood Boulevard back in the fifties, he turned down the honor.

About 30 years later, he reconsidered and became the 1900th star on that sidewalk. But he kept his humility, reminding stargazers, "We should put our eyes on *the* star, which is the Lord."

Honor Your Colleagues

When actress Barbara Stanwyck received an honorary Oscar, she held it up and spoke of her late costar William Holden: "He always wished that I would get an Oscar; and so, tonight, my Golden Boy, you've got our wish."

Recognize Your Competitors

Did you win a state basketball championship? Walk away with the top sales award for your company? Score a much-talked-about victory?

Praise your competitors for their ability, their hard work, their sportsmanship.

Let Your Personality Shine Through

When Bette Davis was honored by the Film Society of Lincoln Center, she received a standing ovation that lasted more than a minute and a half. After acknowledging the cheering crowd, the actress looked right at those 2,700 Davis fans and gave them a bit of the acid wit they had come to love over the years.

"What a dump!" she said, bringing down the house with her well-timed delivery of that classic Davis line.

Try Candor

At age 79, Mary Roebling, the first woman to head a major bank, retired as chairperson of the National State Bank. And in her mid eighties, she found herself busier than ever.

Within just one week, she participated in three award ceremonies. She was named U.S.O. Woman of the Year, she presented an award to honor Professional Women in Construction and Allied Industries, and she was saluted by the Daughters of the American Revolution in Trenton, New Jersey.

Ms. Roebling's response? "I keep thinking people are confusing me with someone else."

A Little Humor Can Work Wonders

George Burns knew the value of humor when he received an honorary degree from the University of Hartford at age 92. Burns said, "I can't wait to run home and tell my mother about this. She always wanted me to be a doctor."

Keep It Brief

At 98, Jack Horwitz was honored by the Long Island Medical Center for his role as one of the hospital's founders. Many speakers praised him, but, Mr. Horwitz kept his remarks disarmingly brief: "It's nice to hear everything you said while I'm still alive. I'm glad I'm here. I think I said enough." And so his speech was finished—in about a minute.

When I think of all the audiences that have suffered through long, boring, pompous acceptance speeches, it makes Mr. Horwitz's sincerity and brevity seem all the more noteworthy.

IF YOU'VE LOST

Lose a prestigious award? A big account? An important game? Try to put your loss in perspective.

Yes, you have to acknowledge defeat . . . but no, you don't have to dwell on it. Say you did your best, but acknowledge that the winner did better.

19

Above all, be a gracious loser. Don't be mean-spirited. Let the victors enjoy their moment in the sun.

When Preacher Roe was with the Brooklyn Dodgers back in the forties and fifties he had a favorite saying: "Some days you eat the bear. Some days the bear eats you. Yesterday, the bear ate us."

POSTHUMOUS AWARDS

When people are honored after their death, who's the best person to accept the award in their honor? Quite often, it's a family member. If you are invited to accept a posthumous award on behalf of a relative or a close friend, ask yourself:

• What's the real significance of this award?

• Why is the deceased person being honored?

• How might he or she want to respond to this honor?

• What legacy has the deceased person left?

The American Society of Journalists and Authors posthumously gave an Outstanding Article Award to Laurence Cherry, who died of leukemia two days before his winning magazine article was published. His sister, Rona Cherry, then executive editor of *Glamour* magazine, made a moving acceptance speech:

> My brother would have felt quite humbled—and very pleased—to receive this award from the ASJA. . . . We humans have a great ability to fight and adapt to any change that comes our way. And when we join someone in that fight for life, we sometimes discover that our own capacity to care and love has deepened more than we ever could have imagined.

CHOOSING THE AWARD

Plaque? Trophy? Paperweight? Engraved tray? Monogrammed desk set? The choices are almost endless.

Unfortunately, so are the pitfalls. Before you pick any award, ask a few practical questions. Use this checklist:

_____ *Is it too big to fit into a recipient's briefcase or luggage?* A loving cup might prove awkward for your honoree to carry onto an airplane.

_____ *Is it too fragile to survive a long trip?*

_____ *Is it perishable?* A manager was honored at an out-of-state conference. Unfortunately, she was presented with a basket of regional foods, which spoiled before she got home.

_____ *Will it just collect dust?* A gigantic paperweight might only take up desk space. Something more functional (say, a radio, or a desk set) could be used every day.

_____ *Is it appropriate?* For example, why give a gold watch if you know the recipient already wears a special watch? Maybe a fine pen would be more appropriate.

_____ *Will your cost-cutting measures result in a cheap-looking award?* Every award ceremony has budget limitations. But no matter what your spending cap, make sure your award still looks top-of-the-line. Opt for a small bowl of great quality, rather than a large bowl of mediocre quality.

If you're having the award engraved, consider where you place the inscription. For example, if MAN OF THE YEAR appears on the front of a standing desk calendar, only the honoree will see it. If you place that inscription on the opposite side, all the visitors who sit across the desk from him will see it.

21

BIRTHDAYS

I have declined letting my birthday be known, and have engaged my family not to communicate it.

—THOMAS JEFFERSON

Whether announced or not, birthdays have a funny way of becoming public knowledge.

If your staff throws a coffee-and-cake birthday party for your secretary, or if your father decides to throw himself a 75th bash, or if your boss deserves a few special words on her 50th birthday, could you say something appropriate?

These ideas might help:

WISHING SOMEONE A HAPPY BIRTHDAY

Use a Catchy Quotation

Turn to a good reference book (see the Appendix for some suggestions) and find a lively quote. Maybe . . .

- Sophie Tucker: "Life Begins at 40."

- George Orwell: "At 50, everyone has the face he deserves."

- Coco Chanel at 60: "Cut off my head and I am 13."

Give Some Historical Details That Relate to the Person's Age

For example:

> We're all here to wish our manager a happy 50th birthday. Of course, we're all wondering what surprises he has in store for us this year. After all, Charles Bronson was 50 when he became an overnight sex symbol. Henry Ford was 50 when he introduced some crazy idea he called "the assembly line." And Henry Kissinger was 50 when he won the Nobel Peace Prize.
>
> Now, we don't know exactly what our manager is cooking up for *his* 50th year, but we hope it's something good, and we wish him the very best.

Talk About the Birth Year

Was your principal born in 1950? What were the big events of the year? Who won the Academy Award? What was the number-one best seller? Who made the top news stories? (You can get this information by looking at an almanac, or checking with a reference librarian.)

This historical trivia will capture the audience's interest—and show the honoree that you cared enough to prepare a clever speech.

Go Beyond Words

Sometimes, the best birthday tributes don't use words. Consider these creative approaches:

- When George Delacorte, the philanthropist and founder of Dell Publishing Company, turned 97, the New York City Parks Department wanted to salute him for the wonderful things he had given to the city's parks over the years. Their special tribute? A rendition of "Happy Birthday" played on the animated animal clock that bears his name at the Central Park Zoo.

- When Queen Elizabeth, the Queen Mother, turned 90, plans for a military parade were scrapped in favor of a less traditional parade—a parade that would include an Aberdeen Angus bull, six chickens, and a pack of dachshunds. Why the animals? They represented some of the 300 organizations of which the Queen Mother was a patron, including the Poultry Club, the Dachshund Club, and the Agricultural Society of Scotland.

CELEBRATING YOUR OWN BIRTHDAY

I'm 53 years old and six feet four. I've had three wives, five children, and three grandchildren. I love good whiskey. I still don't understand women, and I don't think there is any man who does.

—JOHN WAYNE

Can't imagine what you'd say if someone threw a big birthday bash in your honor?

Here's how some people approached their birthdays:

Play a Mathematical Game With Your Age

James Thurber once said, "I'm 65, and I guess that puts me in with the geriatrics, but if there were 15 months in every year, I'd only be 48." Alas, Thurber was better at comedy than math: if a year had 15 months, he'd have been 52! But still, you get the idea.

Express Satisfaction With Your Family

Lord Lytton once said, "At 60, a man learns how to value home." You could build on a quotation like that to express the joy you receive from having a wonderful family, the satisfaction you take from relaxing in your own home, the pleasure you get from working in your garden.

Acknowledge the Advancing Years

Not so young as you used to be? No one is. But, listen to Rose Kennedy's spunky comment on her 100th birthday: "I'm like very old wine—they don't bring me out very often, but I'm well preserved."

Try a Little Humor

For example, I once gave this quip to a client to use at his 50th birthday party:
"Gore Vidal once said, 'For certain people, after 50, litigation takes the place of sex.' Well, I hate to disappoint all the lawyers in this town, but . . ."

Poke Fun at Your Image

When Prince Charles turned 40, he sported a LIFE BEGINS AT 40 button and poked fun at his image as an eccentric. The prince gave a carefully crafted speech that mocked his tabloid image as a kooky person who talks to plants:

Only the other day I was inquiring of an entire bed of old-fashioned roses, who were forced to listen to my demented ramblings on the meaning of the universe as I sat cross-legged in the lotus position . . .

His self-parody brought cheers from the 1,500 youths who were invited to celebrate the prince's birthday.

Find Advantages in Growing Older

Perhaps something like this:

Jean Renoir, the French film director, once said, "The advantage of being 80 years old is that one has had many people to love." Well, that's true. And, when I look around and see all of you at this party, I'm grateful for the family and the friends that *I've* been able to enjoy these 80 years. I love you all. And I thank you for giving me such a happy birthday.

Tap the Wisdom of Your Years

Pearl Buck made these comments in her 80th year:

Would I wish to be "young" again? No, for I have learned too much to wish to lose it. . . . I am a far more valuable person today than I was 50 years ago, or 40 years ago, or 30, 20, or even 10. I have learned so much since I was 70. I believe I can honestly say that I have learned more in the last 10 years than I learned in any previous decade.

If You're Caught By Surprise . . .

You're working in your office, you hear a little commotion outside your door, you look up—and all your cronies have gathered to surprise you with a birthday cake.

Might as well join their spirit of fun and respond with something funny. A manager I know got a surprise from her staff when they serenaded her with a birthday cake blazing with 50 candles. Her good-spirited response? "Well, getting older may not be so great, but it sure beats the alternative. Thanks for thinking of me!"

No one expects you to give a real speech under these circumstances. A smile and a simple lighthearted response will carry the day.

BUILDING DEDICATIONS

GROUNDBREAKING; CORNERSTONE LAYING; OPENING DAY

A city, in its most real sense, is its buildings. Whatever the life, spirit, activity or achievement of the city may be, they are expressed in the mass of asphalt, brick, stone, marble, steel and glass that has accumulated during the city's existence.

—ADA LOUISE HUXTABLE

The county builds a new library. The university dedicates a new monument. The state opens a new park.

If you're the person who's responsible for saying a few words at the dedication ceremony, ask yourself some basic questions before you prepare your remarks:

Who Cooperated on the Project?

Find out the names of key leaders, planners, and supporters, and thank them for their cooperation. For example:

> There's a Roman proverb that says, "A strong city can only be built by brother helping brother." And that was certainly the case when we built this new YMCA for our community. Many people helped to turn our dream into reality, and I'd like to thank them now.

Notify those people in advance, so they're ready to raise their hands or stand up when their names are mentioned.

28

Who Will Attend the Event?

Publicists like to joke, "Give me a couple of weeks, a couple of spotlights, and a couple of celebrities, and I can make a grand opening for just about anything."

The mere presence of some "big names" will create special interest for your ceremony. Know who will attend, what they're famous for, how they contributed to the effort. Think about why they're important to the community, and how they can serve as role models for the audience. Mention a few of these details in your speech.

Will Anyone Else Speak?

I once attended the dedication of a civic center where one of the officials seemed to forget the presence of other speakers. While he rambled on for 25 boring minutes, the audience became increasingly restless—and the other speakers became increasingly worried.

Thou shalt not steal another speaker's time.

Is There a Suggested Theme for the Event?

Will the ceremony revolve around a central theme? Will it be tailored to a specific public relations objective? If so, you'll want to know about that.

Try to be more profound than Calvin Coolidge was on one occasion. When the president was asked to break ground for a public building, he merely pointed to the broken earth, said "That's a mighty fine fishworm," and left.

Chances are, your audience will expect something more substantial.

Will a Plaque or Other Memento Mark the Dedication?

Two years after the *Challenger* disaster, the space shuttle *Discovery* was moved to Cape Canaveral's launch pad in an upbeat ceremony designed to boost confidence and pride in America's space program.

Lieutenant Colonel David Hilmers of the Marine Corps told the cheering July Fourth crowd, "It is a mark of a great nation, of its greatness, that it can rise again from adversity. And with *Discovery*, rise again we shall."

Then Colonel Hilmers was presented with an autograph book that was to accompany the *Discovery* crew on its voyage. The book contained the signatures of 15,000 space agency employees who worked to support *Discovery* "from lift-off to landing."

What Does the Building Represent to Your Community?

Buildings are more than bricks and mortar. They're a reflection of the community they serve. When Dr. William Vincent, president of Bucks County Community College in Pennsylvania, spoke at the dedication of that county's new library, he stated:

> The facility we are dedicating today is a monument to what Bucks County stands for. . . . It is a monument of good bipartisan leadership over the years. It is a monument to our fellow citizens who support the life of the mind through their participation, as well as their tax dollars. It is a monument to the human spirit that prevails today among us all and is forever recorded in this repository.

How Will the People in Your Community Be Helped?

Will your new library boost literacy? Will your new retirement center give seniors more dignity? Will your new community swimming pool teach kids to become better, safer swimmers?

Always point out the *human* benefits of any construction efforts. As Winston Churchill once said, "We shape our buildings; thereafter, they shape us."

What High Purpose Will Be Served?

When Steven Beering, the president of Purdue University, spoke at the School of Education inauguration, he emphasized the importance of education:

> Education is dreaming, and thinking, and asking questions. It is reading, writing, speaking, and listening. Education is exploring the unknown, discovering new ideas, communicating with the world about us. . . . Education is unfinishable. It is an attitude and a way of life. It makes every day a new beginning.

Has the New Building Been Well Received?

If the librarians were pleased when 1,000 people checked out books on the first day, say so.

If the swimming coach was pleased when 300 kids signed up for swimming lessons at the new pool, say so.

If the curator was pleased when 500 people attended the museum on opening day, say so.

After all, nothing succeeds like success.

What's Important About the Name?

At the dedication ceremony for Canada's Walter L. Plonski Forest, the Honorable Vincent Kerrio, Ontario minister of natural resources, said:

> At a time when Ontario's forests are under close scrutiny, it is important to bring some perspective to our studies. Some people think our forests have endured *despite* man; I believe they have endured *because* of man—because of men like Dr. Walter Plonski.
>
> Today we are honoring a true pioneer. Dr. Plonski laid the foundation for forest management planning in Ontario, right here in this forest, more than 25 years ago . . .
>
> When I asked his colleagues how they would sum up Dr. Plonski's work, I was inundated with superlatives. . . .
>
> Rarely does one encounter a person whose professionalism and personality inspire such deep feelings of loyalty, admiration, and outright affection. . . .
>
> I hereby name this the Walter L. Plonski Forest.

What Are Your Personal Feelings?

At the dedication ceremony for J.C. Penney's Manhattan headquarters, founder James Cash Penney shared his personal feelings: "I wouldn't be human if I didn't feel pride and something that transcends pride—humility."

Well said.

CHILDREN'S GROUPS

Kids in the first grade will be looking up to you, so watch what you say or do.

—COUNTRY SINGER REBA McENTIRE, AT A TENNESSEE GRADE SCHOOL
COMMENCEMENT

You're a police officer, and you'll be visiting local schools to talk about drugs. You're a businessperson, and you'll be speaking at "Career Night" at the local junior high school. You're a parent, and you'll be talking to Girl Scout troops about a special volunteer project.

How can you get your message across to *kids*?

Use Language That Kids Can Understand

When President Bush initiated an antidrug campaign, he made a special effort to reach kids—who are so very vulnerable to the nation's drug epidemic.

His method for reaching millions of young people? A televised speech that brought his antidrug message into classrooms and assemblies all across the country.

Using simple, everyday language, Bush said that "saying no to drugs won't make you a nerd."

Use More Than Just Words

Kids like things they can see, touch, taste, smell, and hear for themselves. So try to bring along some props that will grab their attention.

33

For example, when Bush gave his antidrug speech to school kids, he displayed the badge of a 22-year-old rookie policeman who was killed while protecting a witness in a drug case. He said, "To me, this badge is a constant reminder that Eddie Byrne's life was not given in vain." Other examples:

- A woman who lectures on wildlife takes an injured owl into the classroom with her. When children see how pesticides blinded this magnificent creature, they not only listen to her message, they remember it.

- A park ranger who talks to kids about environmental issues takes "mystery boxes" into classrooms. Blindfolded kids put their hands into these boxes and try to identify the objects they're feeling—perhaps seed pods, moss, wheat, a dandelion stem.

Be Approachable

Using a lectern might be fine in a large auditorium, but in a small classroom, it will just create an unnecessary barrier between you and the students.

In fact, if you're talking with small children, you might prefer to sit. Talking at their level will make you seem less intimidating and more approachable. You might want to have the children sit in a circle so everyone has a good line of sight and feels included.

Vary Your Pace

Kids get restless easily, and they're not the least bit embarrassed to show their boredom. So plan a variety of examples, demonstrations, and explanations. If your first effort fails, at least you've got a backup.

Allow Plenty of Time for Questions

Chances are, your listeners will have a host of questions and comments. If you overplan your presentation, you'll deprive them of the opportunity to take part.

Treat Kids With Respect and Kindness

As one first-grader once told me, "I may be little, but I'm a person too." And right she was.

Listen to children's comments with respect. Don't be patronizing or bossy; it will just turn kids off.

Be friendly and kind. It was John Ruskin who observed, "Give a little love to a child and you get a great deal back."

COMMENCEMENTS

The human mind is like an umbrella—it functions best when open.

—WALTER GROPIUS

You answer the phone and it's the alumni director from your alma mater, asking you to speak at the next commencement ceremony.

You're flattered, of course. It's quite an honor; probably the most prestigious speaking invitation you'll ever get.

You're excited, too. Thousands of students, parents, professors, administrators, reporters—probably the biggest audience you'll ever face.

And, truth be told, you're also a little nervous. After all, commencement speeches don't come along every day. So even if you're an experienced speaker, you probably haven't had an opportunity to give a commencement address. And that alone can create anxiety.

Well, relax. This is a perfectly normal reaction. Just take everything step by step, and you'll gain one of the most satisfying speaking experiences of your career.

BEFORE YOU DO ANYTHING

Before you pick a topic, before you do any research, before you write one word of your speech, ask some basic questions about the commencement ceremony.

This list of questions will give you a better understanding of your role at the graduation event:

1. *Will there be any other speakers?* Most ceremonies feature one major commencement address; others feature several short speeches. If you're one of several speakers, ask to speak first, before the audience

becomes fidgety. And find out what the other speakers will discuss, so you can avoid overlap.

2. *How long should I speak?* Use the university's guidelines, but take them with the proverbial grain of salt. If they've asked you to speak for 30 minutes, disregard their suggestion. That's too long. Instead, prepare a lively 12- to 18-minute speech, and you'll be a hit. Whatever you do, *don't* run on too long.

3. *Who will introduce me?* Send that person a completely written introduction—not a bio or a résumé, but a smoothly written introduction that's specifically tailored to your commencement address. You can learn how to do this in the Introducing Speakers chapter (see page 71).

4. *Will the ceremony have any special highlights?* Honorary degrees? Academic awards? Posthumous presentations? You might want to incorporate these details into your theme.

5. *What's unique about this commencement?* Is this the first commencement for the new college president? The last ceremony before a popular dean retires? The largest graduating class?

6. *Are there any related activities I'll be asked to attend?* Commencement speakers are often honored at special luncheons, cocktail parties, and receptions. Find out the timetable so you can make appropriate travel plans.

CREATING A MEMORABLE SPEECH

A commencement is a big event, filled with fine achievements and noble aspirations and grand emotions, and your speech must match the occasion.

Take the high road. Make your audience *feel* good. Give them something to remember with affection and with pride. Use these ideas for inspiration:

Salute the Parents

Parents put a lot of thought and care and—lest we forget?—*money* into their kids' education.
Salute their efforts. *Profusely.*

Praise the College

Desmond Tutu, the Anglican archbishop of South Africa, praised Wesleyan University for supporting black liberation in his country. In particular, he praised Wesleyan for backing economic sanctions against South Africa's racist, minority government.

Ask the Graduates to Choose a Better Future

New Jersey governor Tom Kean, speaking at Fairleigh Dickinson University:

> You've all had it drummed into your heads—often by some of the disillusioned dreamers of the sixties—that getting ahead in the world is all that matters.
> But I ask you, what kind of a world do you want to succeed in? Do you want to be a success in a world where genocide still goes on, where thousands of your fellow citizens are still homeless, and where children have to be fingerprinted in case they disappeared?
> If your answer is no, then what can you do about it?

Cite the Opportunities of the Future

Ambassador Yuri Dubinin of the Soviet Union said this to the graduates of George Washington University's Elliott School of International Affairs:

> For the first time, mankind now has a chance to rid itself of the ideological, political and military confrontation among states. . . . To quote President John F. Kennedy, "There is a new world to be won."

Encourage Students to Make Bold Changes

Victor Kiam, chairman of Remington Electronics, Inc., speaking at Bryant College:

> What you are, our country will be. You have an absolutely idealistic opportunity to change the world for the better.

Highlight Civic Responsibility

Congresswoman Patricia Schroeder (Democrat; Colorado), speaking at Simmons College:

> [The eighties have] been a decade where the trilogy was me, myself and I. We've got to start thinking about us, our community, our country—and how we are going to compete. There's never been a time when our country needs you more.

Stress Human Relationships

Barbara Bush, giving the speech of a lifetime, at Wellesley College:

> At the end of your life, you will never regret not having passed one more test, [not] winning one more verdict, or not closing one more deal. You *will* regret time not spent with a husband, a child, a friend, or a parent.

Well said—and well received.

Encourage Graduates to Remain True to Themselves

When my alma mater, Millersville University in Pennsylvania, asked me to return to campus to give the commencement address, I encouraged students to be proud of their unique talents:

> Remember who you are. And don't pretend to be anyone else.
> There was an 18th-century rabbi by the name of Zusha. A very wise man. And Rabbi Zusha used to say, "If they ask me in the next world, 'Why were you not Moses?' . . . I will know the answer to that question. But if they ask me, 'Why were you not Zusha?' . . . then I will have nothing to say."
> So remember who *you* are. And don't pretend to be anyone else.

I then cited Barbara Bush and Lady Bird Johnson, who earned our nation's affection and respect by remaining true to their own values.

DOES THE COLLEGE HAVE A UNIQUE STUDENT BODY?

Is the college all female, or does it have an international mix, or is the graduating class composed of nontraditional students? Then speak about the characteristics that make these students special achievers.

For example, when New York Governor Mario Cuomo spoke at the State University of New York at Stony Brook, he discussed the recent rise in racial and ethnic conflict in New York, and then suggested that the diversity of the Stony Brook student body might provide a lesson:

> This is a community that draws students not just from Long Island, but from France, Poland, China, Italy, Israel, Peru, and Vietnam. You're showing all of us how we can live together by learning more about one another.

TROUBLESHOOTING

Okay. You've analyzed the audience. You've prepared a fine speech. You've practiced for weeks. Nothing can go wrong, right?

Well, not exactly. Lots of little things can go wrong at a commencement. If you're not able to deal with them, they might prove unsettling.

And sometimes (I hate to tell you) even *big* things can go wrong. When Mayor Ed Koch gave a commencement speech at the Polytechnic Institute of New York, fire broke out. As the school band broke into a stirring rendition of "New York, New York"—accompanied by the screech of fire sirens—about 3,000 people, including many in flowing academic robes, had to file out of the building through thickening smoke.

Of course, most commencement pitfalls aren't so dramatic. But you should still try to prevent as many glitches as possible. Scan this list of common pitfalls.

Problems With Caps and Gowns

We've all heard of commencement speakers who, en route to the lectern, stepped on the hems of their gowns and unceremoniously tripped. Or speakers who, in the middle of a dramatic gesture, felt their hats slip off.

All sorts of cap-and-gown horror stories can be prevented by providing the college with proper measurements, by arriving early to dress, and by carrying some safety pins and hairpins, just in case.

Problems With Microphones

Find out who's in charge of the sound system, and *get friendly with that person*. Ask, cajole, or even tip that person to stay nearby as you deliver your speech. Seriously.

Problems With the Media

Reporters may try to buttonhole you for an interview before the ceremony. Don't allow this to happen. You need to concentrate on your speech, and you don't want to be distracted by an interview.

Look reporters firmly in the eye and say, "I'll be happy to answer any of your questions—after the ceremony."

Of course, they may persist. They may tell you they're on a tight deadline, they may tell you they'll only ask a couple of questions, they may tell you they'll only take a few minutes. Blah blah blah.

Do not be moved. Stand firm. Say you'll be glad to meet with them *afterward,* and then turn away.

Remember, your top priority is to give a terrific speech for the thousands of people who have come to this commencement with great expectations. You simply cannot allow yourself to be distracted in those precious prespeech moments by one aggressive reporter who wants an interview.

Problems With the Weather

Outdoor ceremonies are nice—until dark clouds begin to form.

When heavy rain fell at a Columbia University commencement, President Michael Sovern suggested that the degrees be conferred all at once, just to speed things up. His suggestion was met with loud boos by graduates, who wanted to receive their degrees in the traditional fashion. So, Dr. Sovern capitulated and agreed, "All right, let's do it the regular way.". However, when Dr. Sovern decided to cut his speech short, the wet crowd heartily approved.

Lesson: Be prepared to offer a shortened version of your speech if stormclouds dictate.

A FINAL CAUTION

Gowns are hot. Folding chairs are uncomfortable. Sound systems can be poor. Ventilation can be nonexistent. Under these less than desirable circumstances, sorry is the commencement speaker who gives a long, boring speech.

If you can't give the world's most fascinating speech, at least you can give a short one.

Albert Einstein was not known for being a stimulating speaker, but he knew enough to keep things short. Einstein once told a commencement audience, "I do not have any particular thoughts to express today, so I wish you all success in your future years." He then sat down.

Maybe there's a lesson in that.

EULOGIES

David Hume
Born 1711
Died 1776
Leaving it to posterity to add the rest.

—EPITAPH OF DAVID HUME, WRITTEN BY HIMSELF IN 1775.

THE TOUGHEST ASSIGNMENT

Common situations:

- A senior executive dies, and the company's CEO is asked to say a few words at the memorial service.

- A much-loved parishioner dies, and the minister is expected to give a particularly moving eulogy.

- A high school principal dies, and the president of the PTA wants to pay a fitting tribute.

- A prominent citizen dies, and the mayor is asked to offer some personal recollections at the funeral.

- A popular employee dies, and the company president wants to say something inspirational.

Can they do what's expected of them? Can they prepare an effective eulogy—one that's consoling, inspirational, memorable? Can they organize their thoughts under deadline pressure? And can they deliver their tribute under the emotional stress that accompanies a death?

Too often, the answer is no. Eulogies rank among the toughest assignments for speechwriters, clergy, and lay people alike.

A tough businessman once told me, "I've spent all my life standing up to shareholders and customers . . . and I always held my own. But when I had to give the eulogy for a coworker, I thought I was coming apart."

He's not the only one who feels insecure under these circumstances. Even experienced clergy often feel inadequate to give a fitting eulogy.

A minister confided to me, "I once had an older person in my congregation who was so popular and so successful that I dreaded his demise for years. I just didn't think I could offer a eulogy that would do justice to this man. And you know what? When he *did* die, my worst fears came true. I really didn't do a very good job, and I'm sorry to say my eulogy didn't begin to pay tribute to this magnificent man."

If you ever have to prepare a eulogy, I hope these examples will help you to do a better job.

Stress Unity

When Ryan White died of AIDS-related illness, the Reverend Raymond Probasco saluted the teenage boy's courage and united his admirers with these remarks:

> Ryan and his family always believed there would be a miracle. But that didn't happen. I believe God gave us that miracle in Ryan. He healed a wounded spirit in the world and made it whole.

Admit the Pain of the Loss

Rabbi Robert Schreibman offered these words at the funeral of eight-year-old Nicholas Corwin, who was slain in a rampage in a Chicago suburb: "So deep is our sorrow, so great is our loss, that we know that God is weeping."

45

Emphasize the Person's Value to the Organization

Vernon Nunn was a beloved administrator who worked at the College of William and Mary for nearly 40 years. Upon Nunn's death, James Kelly, assistant to the president, offered a eulogy that began:

> It would be extremely difficult to speak of Vernon L. Nunn and not think of the College of William and Mary. And it's going to be equally difficult to speak of the college and not think of Vernon Nunn. To generations of students, faculty and staff, the two are inseparable.

Draw on Religious Faith

When Dan Ammerman, a communication consultant from Stafford, Texas, spoke at a friend's funeral, he wove a biblical quotation into the eulogy:

> We gather today to honor the memory of Bob Stottlemyer, who passed to the Lord's care last Sunday. It is written in Matthew, chapter seven:
>
>> Ask and it shall be given to you;
>> seek, and you shall find;
>> knock, and it shall be opened to
>>   you;
>> For everyone who asks receives,
>> and he who seeks finds,
>> and to him who knocks it shall be
>>   opened.

I don't think Bob had to knock. I think as his hand reached for the door to eternal life, it swung open.

Remember the Person's Kindnesses

Jonathan Segal, editorial director of Times Books, shared this story when he spoke at the memorial service for Joe Consolino:

> A few years ago, several of us working for Joe made presentations at an always important sales conference. After we had finished, we went off to celebrate, and unusually, Joe did not join us. Only later I learned why: he had been told that the company he had rebuilt, that he was so proud of, was to be sold. The news must have devastated him. His future was uncertain, but he was already working feverishly to ensure that all of us would be provided for; he had no time for a celebration that day.
>
> But, he did have time to do a little shopping. When we returned to the office from the post—sales conference celebration, each of us found a box of chocolate on our desks, with a note inside. It read, "Thanks—you did good." And it was signed, "Joe."

Talk About How Much You Miss the Person

At a memorial mass on the 20th anniversary of the assassination of President Kennedy, brother Ted Kennedy included these thoughts in his tribute:

> Inevitably we cannot forget the pain of his loss. On bright summer afternoons at Cape Cod or in this waning season of the year, how often we still think of him in all his vigor and say to ourselves, "We miss you, Jack, and always will."
>
> But in the darkness, we see the stars, and how clearly we see him now. We have known other great men and women in our time, in other countries and our own. Yet there was a spark in him so special that even his brief years and early passing could not put it out.
>
> He made us proud to be Americans, and the glow of his life will always light the world.

47

Stress Family Ties

When John McCloy died after having spent a life's work in public affairs, he was eulogized by international leaders in law, finance, and government. But the speeches didn't just focus on the achievements of Mr. McCloy's impressive career.

Mr. McCloy's young grandson, Rush McCloy, described his grandfather as a "loving, caring man who always had a lap to crawl into." Best of all, the grandson said, "if Dad and Mom said no, I only had to ask Big Poppa."

Speak Directly to the Deceased Person

When Iphigene Ochs Sulzberger, successively the daughter, wife, mother-in-law, and the mother of publishers of *The New York Times*, died at age 97, her granddaughter, Susan Dryfoos Selznick, spoke on behalf of the family. She addressed her grandmother directly, saying:

> You were particularly important to these men, who carried on the tradition of *The New York Times*. It was said you were the "hidden power" behind the paper. I remember asking you if that was true, and you said, "Who am I to deny anything nice that people have to say about me?"
> And then you winked.

Reminisce About Early Years

When the FBI confirmed that Marine Lieutenant Colonel William Richard Higgins was probably killed by his Shiite Moslem captors in Lebanon, his wife, Marine Major Robin Higgins, cautioned against anger and said, "Now is the time to tell Rich Higgins that we love him and miss him."

Recalling that her husband wrote in his high school yearbook that his goal was "to always make my family proud of me," she added, "He succeeded."

Share an Anecdote

Choose a story that reveals the person's character.

A host of patrons and friends came to pay their respects to Frances Steloff, the legendary founder of the Gotham Book Mart in New York City, who died at 101.

Roger Straus, president of Farrar, Straus & Giroux, offered this insight into Ms. Steloff's bookselling career: "Frances always had some book or author she wanted to press on you. She was not above saying, 'Buy a copy of this book. The author needs the royalty.' "

After a pause, he added, "It's a practice I approve of."

Quote the Deceased

When famous faces from the world of fashion, art, and publishing gathered at the Metropolitan Museum of Art to pay tribute to the legendary fashion figure Diana Vreeland, photographer Richard Avedon brought the house to laughter with this Vreeland quote:

> She used to say, "I know what they're going to wear before they wear it, what they're going to eat before they eat it, and where they're going to go before it's there."

Share Some Literature That Has Special Meaning for the Family

Senior naval officers, members of Congress, and about 1,000 other people gathered at the National Cathedral in Washington to pay final respects to Admiral Hyman Rickover, founder of the nuclear navy.

Mrs. Rickover had asked former president Jimmy Carter to read from John Milton's "Sonnet on His Blindness."

At first, Mr. Carter said, he was puzzled by the widow's choice. But then he came to realize that the last line of Milton's poem had special meaning for all the wives of submariners who were away at sea: "They also serve who only stand and wait."

Give the Audience a Chance to Smile

Mourners often welcome the opportunity to enjoy some gentle laughter, to recall a funny incident, to remember the good times. By using a light touch of humor, you can ease their grief and unite the mourners in a shared memory.

When Barry Ashbee, assistant coach of the Philadelphia Flyers, died of leukemia at age thirty-seven, the Reverend John Casey, chaplain of the team, said, "The Lord has taken him to his place of rest. Let us hope it is a place where he will see nothing but great defensemen and that the ice will always be smooth."

ECUMENICAL SERVICES

Funerals should aim to unite all of the families, friends, and admirers in a shared spirituality that fosters a common bond.

The memorial service for Admiral Rickover, who was born to a Jewish family in Russian Poland, was decidedly ecumenical. It was held in an Anglican cathedral, with a Roman Catholic priest giving the eulogy, and a Baptist reading an inspirational sonnet. A Jewish, a Protestant, and a Catholic Navy chaplain each lead prayers.

MEMORIAL SERVICES FOR MASS DEATHS

What words of comfort could you offer if several high school students were killed in a car crash on their way to a big football game? If an entire family was killed in a hotel fire while taking a vacation? If a group of senior citizens was killed while making a bus trip?

Mass deaths bring mass grieving, and speakers must take extra care to meet the mourners' emotional needs, to offer a sense of comfort, to provide a sense of community.

Thirty-five students from Syracuse University were killed when Pan Am flight 103 crashed over Lockerbie, Scotland. At a news conference, the chancellor of the university, Dr. Melvin Eggers, said, "We have lost some of our best and brightest. They were talented and beautiful people. It will be hard to express our sorrow."

The university then organized a campus memorial service where more than 10,000 people gathered to share their tragic loss. As speaker Mario Cuomo, governor of New York, explained it, "We gather here because so great a grief cannot be borne without being shared."

In his address, Governor Cuomo shared an inspirational story from the Talmud about a rabbi and his wife:

When the wife told the rabbi that a man who gave her two diamonds had come to take them back, the rabbi agreed that she had to return the diamonds to the man. After all, they weren't really hers to keep. Then the rabbi's wife explained: "Rabbi, the Lord gave us two precious diamonds—two wonderful sons. And now he has taken them back to him." Hearing this news, the rabbi paused as tears came to his eyes, and he said, "The Lord gave and the Lord has taken away."

Throughout his speech, Governor Cuomo kept his eyes on the families who had sustained this grievous blow.

51

As a final farewell, English professor Douglas Unger slowly called the name of each student, ending with this parting: "To all of you, good-bye. Good-bye to our friends and our darlings."

INFORMALITIES

Sometimes, words alone can't express your emotions. Consider:

Music

Music speaks a universal language. Congressman Mickey Leland, who was killed in a plane crash in Ethiopia while aiding the cause of world hunger, was eulogized in a Roman Catholic mass, enlivened by the jubilant sounds of gospel singing and the jazzy strains of a saxophone.

A tribute for Irving Berlin included songs and reminiscences interspersed with film and television clips.

A service for jazz saxophonist Dexter Gordon featured musical tributes instead of the customary eulogies.

Art

At a memorial service for painter Elaine de Kooning, people saw photographs of Mrs. de Kooning taken over a period spanning a quarter century.

Personal Possessions

When 5,000 students and friends attended a memorial mass for Hank Gathers, star forward of the Loyola Marymount basketball team, his teammates paraded through the gymnasium displaying the dead player's jersey.

Candles

At a memorial service for the victims of violent crime, candles were lit in memory of violent-crime victims, and pictures of victims were taped on poster boards near the altar.

Whimsical Touches

At a celebration of the life of Jim Henson, beloved creator of the Muppets, congregants waved colorful foam butterflies on wands. The wands were distributed with the programs, which included a quote by Mr. Henson: "Please watch out for each other and love and forgive everybody. It's a good life, enjoy it."

Applause

John Cardinal O'Connor noted the enormous size of the audience who had come to mourn Joseph Addabbo, the 13-term congressman from Queens.

Walking down from the altar at one point, the cardinal turned to the pew where Mrs. Addabbo sat with her children and said, "You have too many friends here to let this moment pass for the sake of propriety." Then Cardinal O'Connor invited the audience to join in a show of appreciation for the congressman. More than 1,500 people rose, turned toward the casket, and applauded.

A FINAL CAUTION

However you choose to express your grief, do it in a way that honors the full dignity of the person's life.

A wise proverb counsels, "Never speak ill of the dead."

FAREWELLS

Farewell: "A sound which makes us linger."

Maybe you're moving to a distant state, or transferring to a different division, or accepting a job with another company. Maybe your branch manager is relocating, or changing careers, or leaving to raise a family.

You'll want to say a few words of farewell. How can you capture the right tone, and avoid the emotional pitfalls that often accompany such partings?

IF YOU ARE THE PERSON LEAVING

When William Faulkner quit an early job as postmaster, he wrote this less than sentimental farewell:

> As long as I live under the capitalistic system, I expect to have my life influenced by the demands of moneyed people. But I will be damned if I propose to be at the beck and call of every itinerant scoundrel who has two cents to invest in a postage stamp. This, sir, is my resignation.

Well, Faulkner's farewell certainly does have a ring to it, but most of us would probably prefer to make our exits in a less caustic way. Here are some ideas to help you craft a farewell speech that leaves *everyone* feeling good.

Thank the People You've Worked With

When Bishop Theodore McCarrick of Metuchen, New Jersey, was chosen to become the archbishop of Newark, he expressed sincere appreciation to the people of his old diocese: "I thank you for all you have done for me—for your goodness, your faith, your generosity."

Allow Your Supporters to Share the Moment

President Reagan ended his farewell address to the American people with this emotional tribute to his supporters:

> We've done our part. And as I "walk off into the city streets," a final word to the men and women of the Reagan Revolution, the men and women across America who for eight years did the work that brought America back:
> My friends, we did it. We weren't just marking time, we made a difference. We made the [country] stronger, we made the [country] freer, and we left her in good hands.
> All in all, not bad, Not bad at all.
> And so, good-bye. God bless you. And God bless the United States of America.

Express Your Ties to the Area

Consider the honesty of Abraham Lincoln's farewell to the citizens of Springfield, Illinois, as he departed for Washington:

> No one not in my position can appreciate the sadness I feel at this parting. To this people I owe all that I am. Here I have lived more than a quarter of a century; here my children were born, and here one of them lies buried. I know not how soon I shall see you again.

Talk About How You'd Like to Be Remembered

Randy Primas, longtime mayor of Camden, New Jersey, fought back tears as he spoke to a cheering audience inside city council chambers:

Since the news of my impending departure, many of the members of the press have asked me the question, "How do you want to be remembered?" It's not for anything physical but . . . as a mayor who tried to make Camden a better place.

Try Some Gentle Humor

Humor can help diffuse the emotional tension. When Harry Truman left the White House, he quipped, "If I'd known how much packing I'd have to do, I'd have run again."

IF OTHERS ARE LEAVING

Thank Them and Praise Them

Be generous, be specific, be sincere. If someone's work wasn't very successful, try to praise the person's enthusiasm, dedication, or integrity. The point is: when people are leaving, they deserve a good send-off. Find *something* to praise.

As Xenophon said, "Praise is the sweetest of all sounds."

Turn Back the Clock

Are you saying good-bye to an accountant who has served your company since 1975? Take the audience down memory lane by recalling the highlights of 1975, when subway fares were still 35 cents, Tom Seaver was a hot name in baseball, and "Rocky" was the tune on everyone's lips.

Try to get old photographs showing the person's early days on staff; back issues of company publications are good sources. Put together a scrapbook. Include shots of colleagues through the years—the more candid, the better.

Offer Personal Remembrances

Ask the person's co-workers and colleagues for some anecdotes. Include a few of these affectionate recollections in your farewell speech.

Cite Professional Accomplishments

If someone boosted sales, or improved morale, or created new programs, say so. Offer details. For example, if someone instituted a drug treatment program that reduced absenteeism by 25 percent, cite that as a major accomplishment. A few well-chosen details will make a big impression—and create a lasting memory.

Try to Create a Family Feeling

When *A Chorus Line* closed as the longest-running show in Broadway history, Joseph Papp, head of the New York Shakespeare Festival, which produced the musical, walked onstage after the final number and introduced all of the members of the current cast.

Then, one by one, he introduced members of the original cast as they came onstage. He also named the show's creators.

Finally, he said, "This show is dedicated to anyone who has ever danced in a chorus or marched in step anywhere." And, with that, he turned to the casts and asked them to take their final bows.

After a record 6,137 shows, the curtain finally came down on *A Chorus Line*. With Papp's fond farewell, it's hard to imagine a dry eye in the house.

FUND-RAISING

Money is always there, but the pockets change; it is not in the same pockets after a change, and that is all there is to say about money.

—GERTRUDE STEIN

The fact is, fund-raising is now big business. Hospitals, colleges, museums, politicians, churches; they all want to improve their fund-raising efforts.

Perhaps your company is supporting a drive for the United Way, or your college is raising money for a special lecture series, or your daughter's softball team is seeking donations to buy new equipment. How can you persuade people to give to your cause?

Contrast Today's Needs With Yesterday's

When Jerry Johnson, vice president of USWest Communications, spoke at a kickoff meeting for the Phoenix YMCA fund drive, he contrasted the problems of yesterday with the problems of today:

I think most of us here this morning can recall the stress, the strain, and the struggle of growing up.

Who in here doesn't remember doing their homework by candlelight, milking the cows at 4 A.M., trudging through waist-high snow for six miles to school each day. And, even if that never happened, you probably remember telling your kids that it did.

But, for most of us, the pains and the pressures we endured as kids helped us in later life. They gave us strength . . . and taught us values like hard work. . . .

That was yesterday.

Where we faced challenges that strengthened us, kids today

face adversities that can kill them. Where we battled burdens that built us up, kids today peddle poisons that tear them down. Where we worried about passing algebra, many kids today worry about passing through gang territory."

Mr. Johnson then told the audience how they could improve this situation by contributing to the Y.

Emphasize People, Not Materials

Raising money to build a new athletic center? Don't sell the bricks and mortar. Sell the great activities that will take place in the new building.

What will people gain if they contribute to that athletic center? Stress the benefits. Appeal to their own interests.

Try a Touch of Humor

When the College of William and Mary held a fund-raising auction in New York, the auctioneer began by teasing the audience "to spend more than you ever intended"—which they did, raising more than $41,000 in just one evening to benefit the college.

Cite Your Own Contributions

Have you given generously to local historic efforts? The audience might appreciate hearing about your contributions. (For example, why do you care so much about restoration projects? How did you first get involved? What makes you keep giving?)

If you're shy about "tooting your own horn," admit your feelings to the audience.

A church member who had contributed generously on many occasions was asked to spearhead an important new fund-raising drive. She felt embarrassed to talk about all the money she had given to the church, and she candidly admitted her discomfort to the congregation: "I'm uncomfortable speaking about my financial gifts to this church, but I hope you take my personal comments in the spirit they're intended." She then spoke about the joy she received from contributing to a church that had brought her so much solace over the years. The congregation sensed her sincerity and responded warmly to her personal message.

Give a Demonstration

Want to involve the audience in your cause? Don't just *tell* them about the benefits of your organization; *show* them.

As founder and president of Center Stage for Seniors, actor Dominick Chianese often speaks to community groups about his non profit organization, which uses "drama therapy" to enrich the lives of older people.

For a quarter of his speech, he talks about the recreation needs of America's graying population, urging the audience to support more active alternatives to the bingo–bridge–bus trip routine. Then, for the remaining three quarters of his speech, he *demonstrates* drama therapy exercises so the audience can see the therapeutic benefits for themselves.

A tip: If you're going to ask for volunteers from the audience, make prearrangements with someone to participate, just in case no one else raises a hand. You don't want to find yourself in a position where you have to "pull" unwilling volunteers.

SOME CAUTIONS

Avoid Technical Language

I once heard a doctor solicit funds for a new emergency service. He had a terrific cause, but he lost much of the audience by using highly complex medical terminology.

You'll be better off if you put everything in ordinary, everyday language, so ordinary people can understand what you're saying.

Define Unfamiliar Terms

I once heard an activist solicit funds for AIDS research. Unfortunately, she used acronyms throughout the speech—GMHC, DIFFA—and some listeners didn't understand what she was saying. Define each acronym the first time you use it, and don't use so many acronyms that they become confusing.

Avoid Long Sentences and Complex Grammatical Structures

One teacher wrote an elaborate proposal for a new program. Unfortunately, when she gave speeches to drum up interest in her cause, she simply read from that tedious document, turning off audiences with her stuffy, bureaucratic language.

Remember, a speech is designed for the ear to listen to, it's not designed for the eye to read. You've got to keep everything simple, so your listeners can grasp your message.

Taking an elaborate document and reading it out loud does *not* make it a speech. It only makes your audience fall asleep.

Avoid Handing Out Materials While You're Speaking

A priest made the mistake of handing out brochures while he solicited funds for an elder-care center. He then watched in dismay as the audience started reading—and stopped listening.

Distribute supporting materials *after* your speech.

A WORD ABOUT FUND-RAISING GIFTS

Perhaps you'd like to offer gifts to your contributors. Fine—just make sure your gifts are appropriate to your cause. Gifts should enhance your fund-raising message.

Some examples:

- If you're soliciting funds to expand your community library, offer contributors a pair of bookends made from bricks.

- If you're soliciting funds to enlarge your hospital, offer a health-related gift that contributors can use to improve their own well-being. Perhaps you could present donors with a calorie counter, or a chart showing women how to give themselves breast examinations, or an attractive booklet with first-aid suggestions.

- If you're seeking donations to provide housing for the homeless, offer contributors a personal letter of thanks from one of the homeless people who've benefited. Let contributors feel they've really made a difference.

HONORARY DEGREES

I had not the advantage of a classical education, and no man should, in my judgement, accept a degree he cannot read.

—MILLARD FILLMORE, DECLINING A DEGREE FROM OXFORD
UNIVERSITY IN 1855

President Fillmore may have turned down an honorary degree, but most people are thrilled to accept the honor. After all, it sure beats dragging yourself out of bed for 8 o'clock classes and burning the midnight oil for exams.

Once honorees find out they'll have to give an address, however, a few doubts start creeping in. Nagging thoughts, such as, "Is it really worth all the bother? Maybe I should just decline and say I have another engagement that day."

Yes, it really *is* worth all the bother. And, no, you shouldn't try to wiggle out of it.

If you're fortunate enough to be offered an honorary degree, snap it up—even if you *do* have to give a speech before you can claim the academic title!

Maybe these suggestions will help:

Flatter the Institution

When John Kennedy received an honorary degree from Yale University, he praised the institution with these words: "Now I have the best of both worlds: a degree from Harvard *and* a degree from Yale."

Express Deep Appreciation

You're receiving a find and rare honor, an honor that places you in a very select group. Acknowledge the richness of the moment, and express your deep appreciation.

Express Pride in Your Achievements

You're being honored because the university thinks you've achieved a great deal. Share some of the highlights of your career. What's given you the greatest satisfaction? What stumbling blocks have you encountered and overcome? What tips can you share with that eager audience?

A commencement audience will be looking up to you. Give them something significant to focus on.

When Helen Thomas, chief White House correspondent for United Press International, received an honorary degree from Elizabethtown College in Pennsylvania, she spoke fondly of her job: "I have been very privileged to cover the White House with my ringside seat to instant history. No democracy is possible without a free press and a free flow of information."

Try Some Humor

Remember, there's no law that says you have to be pompous. Surely comedian Chevy Chase should get an A+ for the way he accepted his honorary degree at Bard College in New York:

> It's customary for a commencement speaker to dole out advice to the graduates as they enter public life. Well, here I go.
> Avoid fatty foods.
> Avoid smoking and drugs, Bensonhurst, the Gaza Strip, Bungee jumping, humorless people, bad music, fashion, weight training, and hair care products.

Oh, and one more thing.

Never, ever tell the truth. Embellish, patronize, pander; use hyperbole, braggadocio; mollify. But never actually tell the truth. In time, those who know you or who are smart enough will *discern* the truth about you. Your job is to act. Keep the dream alive.

Also, never call me. Thank you very much and congratulations.

IMPROMPTU SPEECHES

It takes three weeks to prepare a good ad-lib speech.

—MARK TWAIN

You know that old saying, "The only sure things in life are death and taxes"? Well, I'd like to amend that: The only sure things are death, taxes, and being asked to give an impromptu speech.

You see, it isn't a question of "if" you'll be asked to speak; it's only a question of "when."

A staff meeting, a PTA meeting, a professional workshop, a town forum, a school board showdown; you show up thinking you'll just listen, and then someone points a finger at you and says, "Susan has some experience with this type of program. Susan, could you stand up and tell us how it worked for you?"

Well, *could* you stand up and give a good impromptu speech? You'd better, because all eyes will be on you, expecting you to say something that's both coherent and interesting.

Of course, if you're smart, you'll think about your impromptu speech *before* you're called upon. Anytime you go to a meeting where there's even the slightest chance that someone might ask you to say a few words, you should gather your thoughts in advance.

Ask yourself some basic questions:

• Who will be in the room?

• What's on the agenda?

• Do I have expertise in any of these areas?

• Are there any controversial topics?

• Who are the scheduled speakers?

67

- What do I know that might interest them?

- What do I know that nobody else in the room knows?

Make some notes about subjects that may come up. (You should be able to anticipate about 75 percent of these issues.) Jot down two or three points about important topics.

See if you can find a startling statistic or a compelling example or a catchy quotation, something you can memorize now, then "pull out of the air" when you're asked to speak.

If you practice your responses in advance, they'll be firmly in your mind, ready to use whenever you need them.

WHEN YOU'RE ASKED TO SAY A FEW WORDS

These seven guidelines should help:

1. *Feel free to pause for a few seconds to collect your thoughts.* Believe me, your silence won't cause the audience to think you're stupid. They'll think you want to give a good answer.

2. *Be decisive.* Once you pick your topic, stick with it. Don't change subjects in midstream.

3. *Open with a general statement.* This will give you some extra time to organize your thoughts, allow you to get used to being on your feet, and allow the audience to get used to your speaking style. If you open with something general—"Alcohol treatment programs do a terrific job helping industry control absenteeism," for example—you'll gain five valuable seconds to compose your response.

4. *Offer just two or three points of evidence.* Don't get bogged down with chronological details. "In May of 1989, or maybe it was June, I'm

not sure, it could even have been July, anyhow it was somewhere around then" is hardly a way to inspire confidence in an audience.

5. *Look at the whole room*—not just at the person who asked you to speak.

6. *Wrap up your remarks with a firm conclusion*—a memorable, quotable line that people can focus on. Deliver it with an air of confidence and finality.

7. *Once you've offered your conclusion, don't amend it.* Don't be tempted to add on. Just stop.

HOW TO AVOID OFF-THE-CUFF DISASTER

Suppose, God forbid, someone asks you for an opinion, some advice, a critique, whatever, and you've never given the subject any thought. You're caught totally off guard. Now what?

If you maintain a sense of poise, your audience will accept almost anything that comes out of your mouth. So, keep your chin up, your back straight, your eyes alert, your voice steady, and give a short, simple answer.

Don't embellish. Don't stammer. Above all, don't apologize. If you start saying things like, "Gee, I feel terrible. I didn't know I'd have to say anything. I really don't know much about this topic. I'm so embarrassed . . ." well, if you say things like that, you'll just make the audience uncomfortable, too.

Maybe you can take some comfort from Abraham Lincoln. After General Lee's surrender was announced, people called for Lincoln to make a speech. The president simply said that he had no speech ready and instead called for a stirring rendition of "Dixie."

Look at it this way: whenever you're speaking off the cuff, no one expects you to sound like you're giving the keynote address at a national convention. Just make a short comment—and quit while you're ahead.

If you're afraid you won't be able to come up with *anything*, then memorize this response right now. It may be a real lifesaver someday:

"I don't know. I'll look into that and get back to you with my comments."

Period.

INTRODUCING SPEAKERS

A man never discloses his own character so clearly as when he describes himself.

—JEAN PAUL RICHTER

Suppose you've been asked to introduce a speaker, and you don't know what to say.

A tough spot? Not really. Just call the speaker and ask for a written introduction—not a basic biography (too general) or a formal résumé (too detailed) or an academic *vita* (too scholarly), but a completely written introduction that's *specifically tailored for that speech*.

Most speakers will be glad to oblige. After all, if they write it themselves, at least they'll get an intro they like!

THE INS AND OUTS OF INTRODUCTIONS

What Should a Good Introduction Include?

A good introduction should include:

• several mentions of the speaker's name

• the speaker's credentials

• the title of the speech.

And it should do this in a friendly, personal way that catches the audience's interest and commands the audience's respect.

71

And an introduction should *not*—repeat, *not*—sound like a résumé. For example, "In 1983, her responsibilities included_____. In 1984, her responsibilities included_____. In 1985 . . ."

An introduction should *not* sound like a rehash of the biographical data that's printed on the program. It *should* give some fresh insight into the speaker's interest and expertise in the field.

What If the Speaker Provides You With an Introduction That's Too Boring, Stuffy, or Technical?

Rewrite it to sound more natural. For example, don't recite a long list of professional memberships. Laundry lists put audiences to sleep. Instead, use a lively anecdote that shows the speaker's professional standing.

Don't confuse your audience by using technical language. Why say "The speaker has been employed in the development, design, and effective utilization of methane recovery plants" when you can say "The speaker has saved our community x dollars by turning garbage into gas."

What If the Speaker Gives You an Introduction That's Too Modest?

Add some material that shows the speaker's unique qualifications. What prestigious groups has she spoken to? What recognition has he received? What articles has she published? How much money has he saved the company? Why is she the best person to address the topic?

The more you can establish the speaker as an expert, the better. Audiences like to think they're listening to a real winner.

Some Do's

- Make sure you pronounce the person's name correctly. Verify it with the speaker. Write it phonetically so you can have a last-minute visual reminder.

- Try to create an emotional bond between the speaker and the audience. Do the speaker and the audience support the same charitable causes or care about the same community concerns? Did the speaker and the audience come from similar backgrounds? Did they have to struggle against the same difficulties? Do they share common values? Now's the time to point out these similarities.

- At the end of the introduction, face the audience—*not* the speaker—and offer the speaker's name with a sense of finality: "We couldn't have found a more qualified landscape architect than Paul Robertson." Then turn directly to the speaker and smile. If you look pleased and confident, some of your pleasure and confidence will rub off, making the speaker's early moments at the lectern less stressful and more successful.

- In formal situations, applaud until the speaker reaches your side, shake hands, and return to your seat.

- In informal situations, sit down as soon as the speaker rises to speak.

- Pay attention to the speaker's opening. It may contain a reference to you, and you'll want to smile or nod in response.

Some Don'ts

- Don't try to outshine the speaker. Let the speaker be the star.

- Don't try to cue the speaker. If you say, "I don't know what Marie will talk about, but I certainly hope she gives us the latest re-

73

sults of her new referral program," and if Marie *hadn't* planned to mention that subject, well, then you've created an awkward situation.

- Don't steal the speaker's material. If the speaker told you some startling statistics last week, don't steal the speaker's thunder by citing that data in your introduction. He might have planned to use it in his speech.

- Don't rely on memory. Even if you've known the speaker for twenty years, nervousness might cause you to forget some important details. Use notes for your introduction.

- Don't ad-lib. When you're at a lectern, spontaneity can turn into stupidity with amazing speed—especially if you're giving the introduction after dinner and you've had anything alcoholic to drink. Stick to your prepared comments.

- Don't make grandiose promises, e.g., "This is the funniest speaker you'll ever hear in your whole life." Usually, that's just when the speaker bombs—and you're left looking like a jerk.

- Don't put pressure on the speaker by making comparisons. I once heard a president introduce a new manager by saying, "Susan has replaced Mike Johnson, who we all know was a terrific speaker. So she's got a hard act to follow." As you can imagine, Susan looked somewhat less than comfortable after that introduction.

- Don't speak too long. When a long-winded chairman introduced humorist Artemus Ward, there was nothing left to say on the subject by the time Ward rose to speak. So Ward began, "The chairman has said all that needs to be said on American Wit and Humor, so instead of speaking on that subject I shall lecture on Indian Meal." And, that's exactly what he did.

- Don't make negative comments. Can you imagine how the British politician Joseph Chamberlain must have felt when the mayor prefaced his introduction of Chamberlain by saying, "Shall we let the people enjoy themselves a little longer, or had we better have our speech now?"

Some Clichés to Avoid

At one time or another, we've all heard:

• "A speaker who needs no introduction . . ."

• "Without further ado . . ."

• "Ladies and gentlemen, heeeeeere's . . ."

Wouldn't it be nice if we never had to hear them again?

Sexist Introductions

How many times have you heard a master of ceremonies say, "And now, I'd like to introduce Mr. John Jones and his good wife, Nancy"?

I've always wondered about that. What, pray tell, *is* a "good wife"? And, if poor John got stuck with a "bad" wife, would the MC feel compelled to announce that too?

Another variation is, "I'd like to introduce Mr. Steven Smith and his very pretty wife, Mary." What is this, a beauty pageant? What would the MC say if Mary had less than cover-girl looks?

I'll bet one thing—if *Mary* happened to be the speaker, that MC would never say, "I'd like to introduce Mary Smith and her handsome husband, Steve."

"The good wife" and "the very pretty wife" are tacky and belittling. They have no place in an introduction.

When You Need to Introduce Yourself

If you're introducing yourself, tie your introduction into the theme of the speech.

- When Congressman Peter Kostmayer gave a brief address before the Democratic Convention in Atlanta, he introduced himself as "a United States congressman from Bucks County, Pennsylvania, one of the most beautiful places in America—and we're fighting to keep it that way." Kostmayer then moved on to discuss the environment.

MASTER OF CEREMONIES

We can't cross a bridge until we come to it, but I always like
to lay down a pontoon ahead of time.

—BERNARD BARUCH

A manager was asked to serve as master of ceremonies at a community event, and he wasn't very satisfied with the way he handled his job.
He later confided, "Being an MC was sort of like having to stand up
and juggle a dozen oranges in front of an audience. I just kept standing
there, fumbling everything and waiting for the whole thing to be over
with."

Well, that might be an extreme reaction, but it certainly contains
an element of truth.

Being a good MC takes a lot of organization, plus a lot of personal-
ity. Unless you prepare carefully and rehearse thoroughly, you're going
to be in for a hard time.

Here are a few practical tips to make any MC's job easier:

1. *Know your role.* What are you expected to do? What image should
   you present? Why were you chosen? What did previous MCs do well
   or poorly? Can you learn anything from their mistakes? Their suc-
   cesses?

2. *Inquire about the speakers and participants.* Will you have to introduce
   other people? (Be sure you know how to pronounce their names correctly.) Does protocol demand that speakers be introduced in a particular order? Who will provide you with proper introductions for the
   speakers?

3. *Ask about the schedule of events.* What time frame must you observe?
   Will participants receive a printed schedule so they'll know the time
   restrictions they must adhere to?

4. *Learn how to handle mealtime logistics.* Will the event include a luncheon or dinner? Must you speak while people are eating? Who will instruct the waiters on the importance of "silent service"?

5. *Inquire about any prizes or awards.* Who will provide those items? Who will distribute them during the actual event? (Without supervision, prizes might "mysteriously" disappear, leaving you empty-handed at presentation time.)

6. *Plan some informal comments.* Comments that sound spontaneous are often prepared well in advance. Think about your role ahead of time, and have a few good lines up your sleeve. And be prepared for the little glitches that often occur: faulty microphones, nonfunctioning air-conditioning, fumbled notes, the clatter of broken dishes. If you prepare a few clever ad libs for these inevitable occasions, you'll be less ruffled—and so will the audience.

7. *Prepare a strong ending.* Don't let the program fade away. Wrap it up—firmly, pleasantly, and on time. Thank the appropriate people. Close with a few strong words that will give everyone a positive send-off.

MEETINGS

A body of people formed to delay progress.

—Anonymous

Boring, inefficient meetings are a legendary part of American business life.

If you would like to join the legions of people who know how to conduct a lousy meeting—one that ruins morale, wastes time, and accomplishes zip—consider these 19 tips. They're practically guaranteed to run any meeting into the ground.

NINETEEN WAYS TO RUIN YOUR NEXT MEETING

1. Pick a Rotten Date

Don't consult a calendar. Don't think about colleagues' work schedules. Don't try to accommodate travel plans. Just plunge right in and pick a date—*any* date. For a role model, emulate the organization that mindlessly scheduled an important meeting for the start of Rosh Hashanah—and then wondered why several key people didn't attend.

2. Pick a Rotten Place

Don't visit any meeting sites in person. Don't demand a comfortable, quiet environment. Just pick a spot—*any* spot. When the hotel manager tells you over the phone, "Hey, you really don't need to come all the way over here to check it out. It's a great room. You can take my word for it"—go ahead, believe it. So what if you wind up next to a marimba convention?

3. Position the Tables and Chairs So Everyone Feels Crowded

If a knowledgeable meeting planner tells you to allow 15 square feet per person for classroom-style seating, just disregard that suggestion. Throw in as many chairs as possible. Don't worry about allowing enough elbow room, so people can put notepads on the tables. After all, if you make the meeting boring enough, no one will want to take notes anyway.

4. Don't Bother to Test the Mike in Advance

It's much more disruptive to wait until the room is filled—at which point you can tap the mike repeatedly and drive the audience nuts by saying, "Is this mike working? Is this mike working? Is this mike working?" If possible, strive to create at least a few screeching sounds in the process.

5. Don't Bother Adjusting the Thermostat

Hotels are infamous for keeping their meeting rooms hot and stuffy. But who cares if the audience falls asleep in the middle of your presentation? They probably won't miss much anyway.

6. Don't Notify the Switchboard

When people call the hotel to ask about your meeting, God forbid they should get a well-informed receptionist who could actually tell them the correct time and location. And while you're at it, forget to put a sign in the lobby. That way, prospective attendees can have the pleasure of wandering endlessly through the halls, looking for an obscure meeting room. And that way, you can have the pleasure of latecomers straggling into your meeting and disrupting everyone's attention.

7. Start Late

Ah, always guaranteed to put people in the right frame of mind, and to set the tone for an efficient, productive couple of hours—or days!

8. Make Sure No One Knows the Real Purpose of the Meeting

Written agendas? Who needs them? Look at it this way: if you don't have a clear-cut goal, at least no one can accuse you of failing to reach it. You can also prepare your own hidden agenda. Then, you can have the satisfaction of slipping stuff past the other attendees.

9. Don't Even Bother Thinking About Who Will Introduce You

When you're busy preparing a presentation, you just don't have time to worry about something as trivial as a proper introduction, right? Oh, well, someone will probably be able to introduce you. Somehow. Maybe. If you're lucky.

10. Don't Worry About Making Your Speech Interesting

People are used to boring presentations. One more won't kill them.

11. Don't Worry About Organizing Your Material

It's easier to ramble. And who knows? Maybe people will mistake your disorganization for spontaneity.

12. Throw in As Many Statistics As Possible

If three statistics would do the job, give 'em 30, just for good measure. That ought to impress them.

13. Don't Offer Handouts

Helpful handouts take a lot of work to prepare. Why bother?

14. Throw Around Generalizations

No need to back them up with any details. Of course, some people might wonder how you came up with your conclusions, but hey, you can't please all the people all the time.

15. Kill the Audience With Slides

Lots and *lots* of slides. Right after lunch. All in a nice, dark room, so people can drift into unconsciousness more easily.

16. Make Negative Comments About Other People's Ideas

That's a sure-fire way to stifle dialogue.

17. Ignore Tough Questions

If anyone doubts your facts, just get huffy. People who don't automatically agree with you can't know much.

18. Allow the Bigmouth in the Second Row to Monopolize the Meeting

You know who I mean: the person who asks a million questions and offers a million comments and never lets anyone get a word in edgewise. Allow this person to jump in with a comment or interrupt with a question whenever he feels like it—even as the rest of the audience grows resentful and impatient.

19. Try to Waste As Much Time As Possible

If a five-minute presentation would accomplish your goals, what the heck, stretch it to 15, so you can look more "impressive." If you run into another speaker's time—tough. If you make the meeting run late—too bad. People love to complain about long, boring, useless meetings. Might as well give them something to complain about, right?

PANEL PRESENTATIONS

Conversation: "The last flower of civilization . . . our account of ourselves."

—RALPH WALDO EMERSON

IF YOU ARE ASKED TO MODERATE A PANEL

- Seat all of the panelists at one time, just a few minutes before the presentation starts. You want to give them enough time to get comfortable and put their papers in order, but *not* enough to become restless or anxious.

- Provide each panelist with a glass of water. (It's better to pour these in advance.) Provide extra pitchers for refills.

- Make sure each panelist can see the clock.

- Make sure the room is comfortable. Find the thermostat and set it back a few degrees, if necessary. The last thing you want is a room that's hot and stuffy.

- Use large name cards to identify the panelists, by their first and last names.

- Start on time. Punctuality has been called the soul of business for a reason.

- Introduce yourself right away. Talk about your interest in the subject. Explain the purpose of the panel presentation. Is it a "first," or an annual event? Are the panelists colleagues or competitors? What makes the subject newsworthy?

- Explain the program's structure: speaking order, number of minutes per panelist, time for rebuttals and questions from the audience, distribution of handouts, sales of books, and so on.

- As you introduce the panelists, use each person's name several times. (See Introducing Speakers, page 71, for helpful tips.)

- Encourage the panelists to take a conversational approach. How would they talk at the office, among colleagues, or at the local coffee shop, among friends? Let the audience feel as if they're eavesdropping on an intelligent conversation.

- Give the panelists a 30-second signal so they can wrap up their presentations on time. One effective technique: display a 3x5 card that reads 30 SECONDS. A visual reminder is less disruptive than a verbal reminder.

- If panelists ignore your 30-second signal, interrupt them politely, but firmly and give them 15 seconds to finish.

- *Do not* let any panelist run overtime. It's unfair to the other speakers, and unfair to the audience. What's more, it undercuts your authority as moderator. In a strong, steady voice, say, "Thank you, Mr. Jones, but your time is up." Do not apologize for taking a firm stand. If any apologies are due, it's the long-winded panelist who should apologize—to you, to fellow panelists, and to the audience.

- Close the panel presentation on schedule with a few words of thanks to the speakers and the audience.

IF YOU'RE A PANELIST

• Prepare for the worst. Inexperienced moderators may not know the above guidelines; lazy moderators may not bother to observe them. Just try to make the best of the situation.

• Ask to speak first. Don't be embarrassed to ask for the best spot; moderators will usually honor your request. If the other panelists didn't know enough to select a good spot on the program—well, maybe they should have read this book.

• Make sure the moderator knows how to pronounce your name. (Don't assume—*ask*.)

• If the moderator forgot name cards or only mentioned your name once when introducing you, start by saying "Hello, I'm_____."

• If the moderator didn't cite your credentials adequately, offer a *brief* biographical sketch. Emphasize the qualifications that apply to your role on the panel.

• If a long-winded panelist refuses to stop speaking and the moderator seems unable or unwilling to control the situation, assert yourself. Slip a note to the moderator. Slip a note to the speaker. If necessary, interrupt: "Excuse me, but you're going overtime, and we're running very late. Out of fairness to the audience, can we move on schedule?" The audience will be forever grateful. And if inconsiderate speakers feel insulted, well, that's their problem.

• If you're the last speaker and time is running out, give a shortened version of your presentation. It's better to give a shortened version and keep the audience's attention than to stick stubbornly to your original version and lose it.

PATRIOTIC CEREMONIES

It is sweet to serve one's country by deeds, and it is not absurd
to serve her by words.

—SALLUST, c. 40 B.C.

Maybe you're a Vietnam War veteran, and you've been asked to say
a few words at your town's Memorial Day ceremony. Or you're the president of a local civic organization, and you've been asked to give a short
speech on Flag Day. Or you're active in community efforts, and you've
been asked to host an Independence Day celebration.

Will you be able to say something patriotic, inspirational, and
memorable? Something that will leave your audience feeling positive
about their town and country?

You can build a variety of patriotic themes around these ideas:

Define Patriotism

Maybe you'll want to quote someone famous. Calvin Coolidge once
said, "Patriotism is easy to understand in America; it means looking out
for yourself by looking out for your country."

Or, maybe you'd rather define the concept in your own words.
What does patriotism mean to you, in *your* community, today?

If you could use a few ideas, ask a child to define patriotism. What
exactly, does the concept mean to your 10-year-old? Kids are wonderfully
candid; you might get a quote that will perk up your whole speech.

Talk About the Flag

Woodrow Wilson once described the American flag as "the emblem of our unity, our power, our thought and purpose as a nation."

What does it symbolize for you?

Maybe you can share some personal recollections. Have you ever fought in battle? When you were a kid, did you help your parents display the flag on holidays? Did you ever march in a patriotic parade? Audiences like it when you share these slice-of-life memories.

Praise Peace

Elie Wiesel once defined peace as "our gift—to each other." If your community faces difficult problems, commit yourself to finding peaceful solutions.

Praise Freedom

When President Reagan gave an Independence Day speech in Decatur, Alabama, he praised America as a land of the free: "No one immigrates to Cuba or jumps over the wall into East Berlin or seeks refuge in the Soviet Union."

Refer to a Nearby Inscription

Does your library, state capitol, or courthouse have an inscription above its entrance? Many do—and they're good starting points for patriotic sentiments.

For example, these words are carved on a plaque at Union Station in Washington, D.C.: "Let all the ends thou aimest be thy country's,

88

thy God's and truth's. Be noble and the nobleness that lies in other men—sleeping but not dead—will rise in majesty to meet thine own."

The following words appear over the doors to the Brooklyn Public Library at Grand Army Plaza: "The Brooklyn Public Library, through the joining of municipal enterprise and private generosity, offers to all the people perpetual and free access to the knowledge and the thought of all ages."

Local inscriptions such as these can create the basis of an inspirational theme.

Praise the Beauty of Your Land

Proud of the rolling hills, the fertile farmland, the majestic mountains? Say so.

Encourage a Broad Outlook

George Santayana once wrote, "A man's feet must be planted in his country, but his eyes should survey the world."

You can use patriotic ceremonies as a time to express cooperation with other peoples.

Foster Unity

Now is not the time for political one-upmanship. Leave party prejudice at home. Concentrate on shared concerns. As New York City mayor Fiorello La Guardia once put it, "There is no Republican or Democratic way to clean the streets."

State Your Pride in Your Government

Stress the positive. In the words of Winston Churchill, "Democracy is the worst form of government that man has ever devised, except for all those other forms that have been tried from time to time."

PRAYERS

Prayer is and remains always a native and deepest impulse of the soul of man.

—THOMAS CARLYLE

Banquets, commencements, award ceremonies, inaugurations, and building dedications often require someone to say a prayer.

If you are asked to give a prayer, can you say something inspirational, gracious, and dignified—something suitable for a public event that recognizes a diversity of religious beliefs?

These seven suggestions should help:

1. Thank God For Your Blessings

A wise Yiddish saying goes, *"Ven me zol Got danken far guts, volt nit zein kain tseit tsu baklogen zich oif shlechts.";* "If we thanked God for the good things, there wouldn't be time to weep over the bad." A public prayer allows you to bring people together by counting your communal blessings.

2. Ask God to Help You Serve Others

When President George Bush delivered his inaugural address to the American people, he said, "My first act as president is a prayer—I ask you to bow your heads." Then he offered these gracious words:

Heavenly Father, we bow our heads and thank you for your love. Accept our thanks for the peace that yields this day and the shared faith that makes its continuance likely. Make us strong to do your work, willing to heed and hear your will, and write on our hearts these words: Use power to help people.

For we are given power not to advance our own purpose nor to make a great show in the world, nor a name. There is but one just use of power, and it is to serve people. Help us remember, Lord. Amen.

3. Pray For Strength During Difficult Times

An old saying goes, "Pray that you may never have to endure all that you can learn to bear." During difficult times, a prayer for strength is both appropriate and welcome.

4. Use an Inspirational Quotation

When evangelist Billy Graham was asked to give the invocation at President Bush's inauguration, he cited this quotation by George Washington: "America stands on two great pillars—faith and morality. Without these, our foundation crumbles."

By quoting the father of our country, Billy Graham tapped into our sense of history and created a shared bond.

Make sure your quotation appeals to a wide cross-section of people. Good choices: bipartisan and interfaith leaders. Their wide appeal will make the entire audience feel included and respected.

5. Commit Yourself to a Noble Cause

Use your prayer to make a commitment, to take responsibility, to move people into action. Heed the advice of Francis Cardinal Spellman: "Pray as if everything depended on God, and work as if everything depended on man."

6. Express a Willingness to Travel in New Directions

A prayer can express your desire to change, to move into new areas, to make a fresh start.

7. Use Candor

Having a rough time? Dealing with some difficult people? Facing a tough situation? Candor may help your prayer cut through the clutter.

After the U.S. Senate finished a marathon session that ran more than 17 hours and exhausted everyone's patience, the Reverend Richard Halverson offered this candid prayer when the Senate returned to work:

> Father in heaven, with unbounded gratitude we praise thee for the incredible political system we inherited from our forebears. It is slow, tedious, inefficient; it tries our patience, sets our nerves on edge, frustrates us, rouses our anger and exhausts us; but we would not trade it for any other system.

A FEW CAUTIONS

Don't Be Stuffy

Prayer has been called "a conversation with God." So keep your language conversational, simple, and easy for the audience to understand.

93

Don't Give a Sectarian Prayer at Public Gatherings

If you give a prayer that's decidedly Catholic, for example, you will make other believers feel excluded—and exclusion is certainly *not* the purpose of a public prayer.

I once attended a civic event where a community leader concluded his prayer by saying, "We pray in the name of Jesus Christ." That sectarian prayer left out people of other faiths.

When Timothy Healy served as president of Georgetown University, he ordered references to the Trinity eliminated from compulsory university functions. His rationale? "If you're going to say a grace over a mixed dinner, why not say one that everyone can join in."

Indeed.

Don't Pray Too Long

Remember, you're supposed to give a prayer, not a sermon. If you make your prayer too long, the audience may become restless. There's an old German proverb: "The fewer the words, the better the prayer."

Don't Use the Same Prayer on Every Occasion

Audiences overlap more often than you might think. If you keep repeating the same prayer at different functions, believe me, people *will* notice. And they will wonder why you don't care enough to prepare something new.

Don't Worry About Giving a "Perfect" Prayer

Perfection isn't your goal; sincerity is. As Gotthold Lessing said, "A single grateful thought toward heaven is the most perfect prayer." Keep that in mind and you'll do just fine.

WHEN WORDS AREN'T ENOUGH

Sometimes the best prayer isn't a prayer. Consider these inspirational options:

Poetry

Perhaps reciting a poem would create the sense of intimacy you're looking for.

Music

When representatives of Jews from around the world gathered at Wannsee Villa in West Berlin, the site where officials of the Third Reich had met decades earlier to plan the Nazi genocide, no prayers were spoken. Instead, participants chanted the Hebrew hymn, "Ma'amin, Ma'amin," declaring faith in the coming of the Messiah.

Silence

Silence is often more eloquent than words. As Bishop Fulton Sheen once said, "Prayer begins by talking to God, but it ends by listening to him. In the face of Absolute Truth, silence is the soul's language."
Amen.

QUESTION-AND-ANSWER SESSIONS

It is better to ask some of the questions than to know all the answers.

—JAMES THURBER

Let's say you've just given a terrific speech. The audience paid attention and gave you a big round of applause. Now that it's over, you can gather your notes, leave the lectern, and relax. Right?

Not so fast. Sometimes, giving a speech is only half the battle; a question-and-answer session might still remain. And if you don't prepare as carefully for your Q&A as you did for your speech, you could be headed for an awkward time.

The fact is, a question-and-answer session can make or break your speech. So plan to make Q&A work for you, not against you.

Here are some general guidelines:

Take Questions From All Parts of the Audience

If you overlook the rear of the room, those people will feel left out. Also, if you take too many questions from one person, everyone else will feel excluded—and annoyed.

Listen Carefully to Each Question

Try to remain neutral as you listen. Avoid excessive smiles or frowns. If you react too soon, you'll upstage your own answer. Some speakers get nervous and nod repeatedly, just to show they understand. Don't do this. The audience might mistake your nodding as a sign of agreement.

Pay Attention to Body Language

If you fidget, the audience will sense your discomfort and think you've got something to hide. Don't play with a pen or jingle jewelry or light up a cigarette. (If you don't trust yourself, remove such items from your person before you speak. After all, you can't click a pen if you don't have one!)

Treat Each Questioner as an Equal

Some speakers automatically respond by saying, "Good question." Don't. After a while, "good question" sounds boring. Even worse, it suggests that other questions *weren't* so good. Also, don't brush off questions from your subordinates and fawn over questions from your superiors. Audiences are quick to spot this attitude—and slow to forgive it.

Repeat All Positive Questions

This way you make sure everyone has heard the question. It also buys you some extra time to compose your answer.

Reword All Negative Questions

This allows you to set the tone and control the emphasis of your answer. *Don't* repeat any hostile language. For example, if you're asked, "Why do you distribute your funds so unfairly?", you could rephrase it: "Is there a better way to distribute our funds? Let's consider that for a moment." Negative questions inflame listeners and make it harder for you to give a balanced answer. And if you repeat a negative accusation, you might be misquoted as having said it yourself.

Begin by Looking at the Person Who Asked the Question

This builds rapport. Then make eye contact with others around the room, as you answer so everyone feels involved.

Respond Simply and Directly

If you make your answer too complex, the audience might think you're trying to evade the issue.

Don't Extend Your Answers

The more you say, the more likely you are to hang yourself. As Calvin Coolidge said, "I have never been hurt by anything I didn't say."

Of course, at times Coolidge carried brevity to extremes. A dinner party guest once asked Coolidge what he did. "I'm the lieutenant governor," he said. "Oh, how interesting," the guest gushed, "you must tell me all about it." To which Coolidge replied, "I just did."

Don't Limit Yourself by Saying, "This Will Be Our Last Question."

What happens if that question turns out to be hostile—or if you give a poor answer? You'd end your Q&A session on a weak note—unnecessarily. It's better to say something like, "We only have a little time left. Any more questions?" Then, if your next question happens to be an interesting one—and if you're satisfied with your answer—you can end the whole session right there. But, if you get a hostile, rambling, or boring question, or if you give a weak answer, you still have the leeway to take another question and try again.

SPECIAL CIRCUMSTANCES

If No One Asks You a Question

Maybe the audience is too shy, too bored, or too unfamiliar with your topic to ask a question. Who knows? But, there's one thing you *do* know: as a speaker, you can't just stand there and let an uncomfortable silence put a damper on your presentation. So ask *yourself* a question. Try, "Earlier today, one of your members asked if I'd address the issue of teacher certification. Let me get to that now." Or, "Last week, when I spoke to the Lion's Club, several people asked me to talk about our funding for the new senior center. That question seems to be on a lot of people's minds, so maybe I should answer it for you, too."

If Someone Asks About Something You Already Addressed in the Speech

Maybe the person was daydreaming; on the other hand, maybe you weren't clear enough! It doesn't matter. Give him or her the benefit of the doubt and answer the question. But approach the topic in a new way so you don't bore the rest of the audience. For example, if you used statistics to illustrate this point in your speech, try using anecdotes or examples to clarify the issue in your Q&A session. If the audience didn't grasp your first approach, maybe they'll understand your second.

If Someone Repeats a Question That's Already Been Asked

Don't answer it. Time is too precious to indulge in this sort of repetition. Say, "I believe we've already taken that question." Then move on.

If Someone Asks a Totally Irrelevant Question

Your marital status, religion, politics, age, finances, your personal life shouldn't concern the audience. If someone hits you with an inappropriate question—"I'm curious. Whom did you vote for in the last election?"—you don't have to answer. In fact, you *shouldn't* answer. Be firm. Say, "That's not what we're here to discuss today." Don't be embarrassed. The person who asks a question like that is the one who should be embarrassed.

When a reporter once asked actress Jaclyn Smith about her financial standing, she dismissed the question quite graciously: "If you're asking me if I'm worth $15 million, I never discuss money. That's my Southern upbringing. We never discuss money, politics or religion." Hear, hear!

If Someone Asks a Truly Inane Question

Give a brief answer—and then go on to another question.

If Someone Asks a Rambling Question

Pick one element and respond to that. (Naturally, pick the element that interests you the most and allows you to give the best answer.)

100

If Someone Tries to Turn a Question Into a Speech

Nip this in the bud. Be polite but firm. Interrupt the person. Ask him or her to come to the point and state the question "in the interest of saving time." When you interrupt the questioner, raise your hand in front of you in a "stop" signal. This gesture will reinforce your words. And believe me, the audience will really appreciate your firmness. Audiences hate it when one person is allowed to monopolize a Q&A session.

If You Don't Know the Answer

Say so. No one expects you to know everything. Try, "I don't know. But I'll go to the source and find out. If you leave me your name and number, I'll be glad to get back to you with that information."

If You Run Out of Time

Say you're sorry the time is up, and offer to make yourself available to people who want to pursue the subject further, perhaps during a break or after lunch.

HOW TO HANDLE TRICKY QUESTIONS

After you've weathered a number of Q&A sessions, you'll be able to spot the tricky questions, and you'll discover they fall into basic patterns. Once you recognize these patterns, you'll handle the questions more easily and effectively.

It took me years of public speaking experience to learn about tricky questions the hard way. In this section, you can learn about them in just a few minutes. Lucky you!

Study the patterns of these tricky questions before you face your next Q&A:

The Hypothetical Question

Avoid being pulled into "what if" situations. For example, "What if you can't meet the deadline?" They're like bottomless pits. Cut off a hypothetical scenario by saying, "We've spent six weeks working on this assignment, and we've met every single deadline along the way. We're confident we'll complete the project on time."

Here's how President Bush handled a hypothetical question during a major press conference on world affairs:

Q: If Mr. Mandela persists in allying himself with a Communist party, would that change your view of his—

A: Too hypothetical. . . . What I'm doing is embracing the concept that it's good that he's out of jail, and that it's good that the South Africans seem to be moving towards a more equitable society.

The Off-the-Record Question

"I know it's not public yet, but would you tell us about your expansion plans—off the record, of course."

Sorry, but there's no such thing as an off-the-record question in a Q&A session. You might think you can trust everyone in the room, but . . .

Assume that any answer you give will appear on the front page of tomorrow's paper. It just might!

The Ranking Question

"Would you name the two biggest challenges facing your corporation?"

If you answer with, "Our two biggest concerns are increased productivity and larger facilities," someone will surely counter with, "What's the matter? Don't you consider minority employment to be a priority?" And then you're stuck in a hole.

Don't allow a questioner to force you into an arbitrary ranking system. Say, "Well, we're concerned with a number of issues right now. Let me tell you about a few of our priorities."

When Eudora Welty addressed the Poetry Center of the 92nd Street YMCA in New York City, she was asked to name her favorite American authors. Miss Welty cleverly sidestepped the question by saying she'd rather read Chekhov than anyone else. Well put.

The Non-Question Question

"I don't see any need for a new training program."

How can you respond to a statement like this without appearing argumentative or defensive? Easy. Convert the statement into a question. For example, "I'm hearing you bring up an important question, and that is, 'Why should we spend all this money on a new training program? What's in it for us?' Then you can answer the question—and cite all the benefits—without having to knock the person's original statement.

The "A or B" Question

"Which will be more important to the company this year: promoting women or promoting minorities?"

Be careful. Don't get tricked into an unnecessary choice. There's no law that says you have to choose between a questioner's options. Say, "They're *both* important. In fact, our personnel department has a few other priorities as well. Let me take a few moments to tell you about them."

Note how cleverly President Reagan avoided the pitfalls of this "A or B" question: When Reagan was asked which team he planned to root for in the world series, he gave everyone a chuckle by saying, "That's an unfair question. I'm supposed to be president of all the people."

The Open Question

"Tell me about your company." This question is deceptively easy—and that's why so many people fail when they attempt to answer it. When given the opportunity to say everything, they can't seem to pick anything. And so they stammer. Or they say something boring. Or they get foot-in-mouth disease.

Open questions are quite common. You get them when you go on job interviews: "Tell me about yourself."

You get them when you go on sales calls: "Tell me about your product line."

You get them when you go to community functions: "Tell us about your company's business philosophy."

Right now, *before* you're put on the firing line, think about some open questions that might apply to *you*—and come up with some good, short, interesting answers. Memorize them. They'll come in handy, I assure you.

The What-Does-The-Other-Person-Think Question

"Why would your competitors be dropping this product line? Do they have something better up their sleeves?"

Unless you are a professional mind reader, you shouldn't speculate about other people's thoughts.

Let other people speak for themselves. Respond by saying, "You'll have to ask them for their reasons." Then bring the subject back into your domain by adding, "But I'd like to tell you why *we're* so committed to this product line."

Consider how President François Mitterand of France handled this type of question. When President Mitterrand paid a visit to Kiev, he said he favored Soviet president Mikhail Gorbachev's proposal for a 35-nation conference on European security, but he wisely avoided speculating on the reactions of the other countries. "I cannot speak for the other 33 countries," he said, "but as for me, I would say if this happened . . . it would be good."

The Yes-or-No Question

"Will you have to fire any employees this year—yes or no?"

Never allow someone to push you into a one-word answer. It's *your* Q&A session, and you can answer any way you want. Make the statement in your *own* words.

HOW TO HANDLE HOSTILE QUESTIONS

He who opposes me, and does not destroy me, strengthens me.

—EDMUND BURKE

Sometimes, a Q&A session will turn nasty.

Let's suppose you're the principal of a public high school, and you've just finished speaking to a community group about the role of parents in education. Your speech went okay, but now a hand pops up and an angry voice hits you with this zinger:

> How can you stand there and tell parents to be more responsible when *you* have failed in your responsibility to us? Ever since you became principal, test scores have gone down, discipline problems have gone up, and salaries have gone *way* up. Where do you get the guts to come here and lecture us about educational responsibility?

Of course, what's really running through your mind at this point is, How can I respond to this question? And the answer is, carefully. *Very* carefully.

Hostile questions aren't impossible to answer. They just take special skills. Why not learn these skills right now—before you find yourself on the firing line?

Start by giving yourself three basic rights:

1. The right to be treated fairly.

2. The right to stay in control—of yourself and the situation.

3. The right to get your message across correctly.

Never forget, *you* are the invited speaker. You are the person who was asked to say a few words to this group. You are the person who spent hours preparing for this Q&A session. And now that you're here, *no one* has the right to take away your role or obscure your message.

106

Take a deep breath, keep your feet firmly planted, and concentrate on getting your message across. Don't focus on the person's anger. Don't focus on your resentment. *Just concentrate on getting your message across.*

When you prepare for any Q&A, choose two or three important points that you can express in clear, simple, concise language—one-liners that you can use whenever you're in a tight spot. Memorize them. Use them as "focus statements" when the Q&A gets difficult.

Here's how three world leaders have handled hostile questions.

- German chancellor Helmut Kohl in an exchange during an interview with *Time* magazine:

Q: Are the Soviets telling you anything bilaterally that they are not saying in public?

A: [laughing] This is not a subject I would discuss with *Time* magazine.

Q: Let me rephrase—

A: You need not continue. I am not going to say anything on that. I know what you were going to ask.

- President Bush, when asked about the possibility of a military response to the reported killing of an American hostage: "We're prudently planning. That's all I've got to say about it."

- President Reagan, when asked about the U.S. reaction to terrorism: "I'm not going to comment on anything that can reveal where we're getting information."

A FEW FINAL CAUTIONS

Don't Insult Anyone's Intelligence

Sorry to say, unthinking speakers do this all the time. Consider this exchange:

Q: Why is the school spending so much money for all that lab equipment?

A: Maybe you don't know what our equipment can do. For example—

Q: Are you saying I'm too stupid to know about your lab equipment?

Don't make the questioner feel stupid or inadequate. Listen respectfully to the question, then say something like, "For the benefit of everyone here, let me just take a couple minutes to explain the equipment in our lab. I'd like to tell you what it can do."

Don't Humiliate Questioners

Try to prevent an exchange like this:

Q: Why didn't you examine the facts more carefully before you planned your budget?

A: *You're* the one who's ignorant of the facts. I guess you must have been daydreaming, because I stated the facts in my speech today. If you'd been listening, you wouldn't have to ask that kind of a question.

Don't browbeat or embarrass questions. They'll never forget the public humiliation, and they'll never forgive you for it. Nor will the rest of the audience.

Don't Make Idle Threats

I once saw a heckler dominate the Q&A session at an important meeting. The speaker grew increasingly frustrated and said, "I'm going to ask you to sit down in a few minutes."

Naturally, the heckler loved all the attention and kept interrupting the session with long-winded questions. The speaker became visibly frustrated, raising his voice and threatening. "I'm going to ask you to sit down soon."

Alas, "soon" never came. The speaker never acted on his idle threats, the heckler kept disrupting the meeting, and the audience became increasingly annoyed—not just at the heckler but at the ineffectual speaker, who couldn't control his own meeting.

If you can't carry out a threat, don't make it.

Don't Criticize a Predecessor's Work

Q: Why do you think your program is so much better than the one Mary Smith started? We've been using her guidelines for years.

A: Oh, the old program had lots of problems, and that's why I had to get rid of it. For example . . .

Don't criticize someone else's work publicly. Even if the person has left the organization, she may have friends who are still around. They will resent you for knocking her work.

The smart response? Explain that you inherited a good program, but that new information, better technology, increased funding, etc., allowed you to build on your predecessor's foundation.

Never give the impression that you've thrown out someone else's work, or the audience will think you are reckless and arrogant.

RETIREMENT TRIBUTES

I had rather be shut up in a very modest cottage, with my books, my family, and a few old friends, dining on simple bacon, and letting the world roll on as it liked, than to occupy the most splendid post which any human power can give.

—THOMAS JEFFERSON, IN A 1788 LETTER

WHEN YOU ARE RETIRING

Perhaps your colleagues will organize a retirement lunch. Or your boss will honor you with a farewell ceremony. Or the president of the company will present you with a special service award.

In any case, you'll be expected to make a few remarks. Since retirement evokes mixed emotions, you might find it hard to respond. These suggestions should help you organize your thoughts and prepare some well-chosen words.

Express Appreciation for the Celebration

Retirement lunches, ceremonies, and tributes require a lot of hard work and planning. Thank the people who cared enough to give you a good send-off.

111

Thank Your Co-workers for Their Support

Remember all those times when your secretary went beyond the call of duty, or your staff worked late into the night, or your boss let you try something new? Well, now's the time to thank them. Be specific. Show that you really *do* remember. And be generous. This is no time to scrimp on the praise.

Turn Back the Clock

Did you join the company back in 1965? Describe the department, the company, the industry in those years. Create a sense of shared history.

Acknowledge Your Mentors

Did a supervisor give you terrific advice, help you through a tough time, or teach you some specialized skills? Now's the time to acknowledge your debt.

Offer Personal Recollections

When General Douglas MacArthur retired after 52 years of military service, he shared these recollections:

> The world has turned over many times since I took the oath on the plains at West Point . . . but I still remember the refrain of one of the most popular barrack ballads of that day, which proclaimed that old soldiers never die; they just fade away. And like the old soldier of that ballad, I now close my military career

and just fade away, an old soldier who tried to do his duty as God gave him the light to see that duty. Good-bye.

Use An Inspirational Quotation

Maybe something like this:

> Someone once said, "Nothing is really work unless you would rather be doing something else." And if that's true, then I guess you could say I haven't really worked a single day these past 30 years, because in all the time I spent with this company, there was never anyplace else I'd rather have worked. And there were never any other people I'd rather have been working with. I will miss you all.

Mention Your Family

When Beverly Sills retired as director of the New York City Opera, she humorously said she planned to vacation with her husband and "see if he can remember what my first name is."

Be Candid

When Walter Wriston retired as chairman of Citibank Corporation, he offered this candid observation: "When you retire, you go from who's who to who's that."

Tell a Lighthearted Story

A little bit of humor can help break the tension that often accompanies a retirement ceremony. For example:

> Two college presidents were talking about their retirement plans. The first president said, "After I retire, I'd like to be a superintendent at an orphanage. No visits from parents!" But the second president said he had a better idea: "After *I* retire, I'd like to be the warden at a prison. No alumni reunions!"

If you look through the books I describe in the Appendix, books I value in my own personal library, you'll find lots of good anecdotes to use in a retirement speech.

Be Direct

When Mayor Henry Maier of Milwaukee retired after a 28-year reign, ending the longest tenure of any big-city mayor then in office, he spoke simply and directly: "I did the best I could with the job. And now it's time to go."

Talk About Your Plans for the Future

Travel? Education? A new sport, hobby, or craft? People will want to hear some details.

Don't just say, "I'll take some college courses." Say, "I've always wanted to visit the Soviet Union, so I'm signing up for Russian studies at our local community college. Marge and I plan to go to Moscow next summer."

Say You'll Stay in Touch

In an emotional farewell address at the 34th Republican National Convention, President Reagan said:

> There's still a lot of brush out at the ranch, fences that need repair and horses to ride. But, I want you to know that if the fires ever dim, I'll leave my phone number and address just in case you need a foot soldier. Just let me know, and I'll be there.

Let People Know That You Plan to Keep Busy

Milton Berle once said, "I don't think you should ever quit working, ever. If you do have to retire, find something else to do." Share your plans for keeping active.

WHEN YOU WANT TO HONOR SOMEONE WHO IS RETIRING

Salute Their Achievements

Don't just praise them, praise them for doing specific things. Otherwise, it sounds like you're just giving a canned speech that you happened to find somewhere.

Be Generous

You have only one chance to create a final impression. This is no time to be stingy with your praise.

Share Some Behind-the-Scenes Stories

People like to reminisce, so take advantage of this opportunity to share a few good stories that will create camaraderie, foster goodwill, and perpetuate fond memories.

Offer a Memento

Now, let me pose a philosophical question: why is it that when people retire and no longer face such demanding schedules, their colleagues generally give them a watch?

Not that there's anything wrong with a watch, of course—the last thing I want is to have all the PR people in the watch business sending me press releases on the value of their product. But maybe, just maybe, you can come up with a few more sentimental ideas. Consider:

- A scrapbook filled with photos, historical trivia, and news clippings that highlight the person's career with the firm.

- A book of humorous "retirement advice," compiled by former colleagues who want to share some of their retirement experiences.

- An audio tape of funny stories, good wishes, and juicy "office tidbits" offered by the staff.

- A videotape; an upbeat montage of familiar faces and scenes.

SALES/INFORMATION BOOTHS

Beat your gong and sell your candies.

—CHINESE PROVERB

Want to hand out literature for your environmental group? Attract customers for your new line of products? Recruit volunteers for your literacy project? If so, you need to know how to run an effective sales and information booth.

A well-run booth is a terrific way to tell people about your organization and gain their support. It's effective, personal, inexpensive, and a great way to keep in touch with the needs of the marketplace, because you receive immediate feedback.

Unfortunately, it can also backfire if you don't prepare carefully. So, use these guidelines as a checklist:

WHAT TO ARRANGE BEFORE THE EVENT

Find an Appropriate Gathering

Some possibilities: community events, professional meetings, college "career days," chamber of commerce exhibitions, trade fairs, conventions, fund-raisers, civic banquets—wherever people gather and have time to linger. Make sure the atmosphere is appropriate for your organization and conducive to conversation. For example, you might be frustrated if you try to run an information booth where alcohol is served or loud music disrupts conversation.

117

Get an Agreement in Writing

Send the organizers a letter of agreement, and ask them to return a signed copy. Why? Because Tom Smith might say, "Sure, you can set up a table at our civic event," but when you get there, someone else might say, "Sorry, no tables allowed." So write a letter of agreement that states your purpose, when you'll operate the table, and where you'll set it up. Be specific. You don't want to be stuck in an out-of-the-way corner. You need lots of passersby to run a successful booth.

Order Sufficient Supplies

Want to give out brochures that describe your organization? Sell copies of your women's club cookbook? Run a bake sale for the PTA? Distribute consumer checklists? Offer samples of a new product? Make sure you have enough materials. There's no sense in operating a table that's half empty. Preparation is crucial.

Schedule Plenty of People to Work at the Booth

Running a booth is tiring—all that talking and standing around. (That's right; *standing* around. If you're seated, you'll seem less approachable. So the cardinal rule is, no chairs allowed!) Since your staff will need breaks every hour or so, be sure you have enough pinch hitters.

Train Everyone Who Will Work at the Table

A well-informed staff will create a more positive impression, so make sure your people can answer a wide range of questions, not just about your organization, but about the entire event. For example, when

118

the University of Pennsylvania celebrated its 250th anniversary, more than 1,000 volunteers got a wonderful training session—enabling them to answer such practical questions as "Where's the toilet?" and "When does the next jitney leave?"

WHAT TO DO DURING THE EVENT

- Always keep in mind that you have a two-part goal: first, you must get people to stop at your booth or table; then, you must get them to listen to your pitch and buy your product or support your cause.

- "Hook" people by having one of your staff stand in front of the table, offering free brochures to passersby. Once people stop to accept your literature, you can generally engage them in conversation.

- You can also hook people by offering a free beverage. Once people stop to drink an icy glass of lemonade or sip a warm cup of cocoa, they'll feel obligated to make small talk with you, and then you've got their attention. If you're worried about the expense, use small glasses or cups. In fact, the small size gives you an extra advantage: as the cup becomes empty, you can offer the people a refill, an act of kindness that should buy you a few extra minutes of their attention!

- Smile and make everyone feel welcome. (That's one of the reasons why a booth is so tiring. You're constantly "on" as you focus all your attention on other people's needs.)

- Use "ringers." If you hit a slow period, station someone in front of your table to browse through your materials. One customer will attract more customers, but an empty table will turn people off.

119

- Don't talk with your partners. If people see you talking, they'll feel you're unapproachable. I once approached a table set up by people trying to recruit volunteers to aid the homeless. The two staff members were so busy chatting with each other that they didn't seem to notice me. I felt uncomfortable disturbing their private conversation, so I slipped away and came back ten minutes later. Again, they were having such a grand time talking with each other that they were oblivious to me and other prospective volunteers. That kind of behavior is foolish and costly. If passersby don't feel welcome at a table, they simply won't linger. And you'll lose a golden opportunity.

- When people seem interested, offer them envelopes and ask them to write down their names and addresses. It will then be easy for you to send them more information.

- Be sure to get business cards from people. Make comments on the back so you can remember key points about each prospect. For example: "Just joined the firm two months ago," or "Wants to improve her visibility in the community," or "Went to Temple University." Record as many details as possible on each card. These bits of information can serve as conversation openers when you make follow-up calls later on.

- Never leave a table unattended. You might lose the chance to make a personal connection. And sorry to say, you might also lose your materials. Things such as pens, notepads, and staplers have mysterious ways of walking off. So be visible and alert throughout the event.

WHAT TO DO AFTER THE EVENT

- Follow up.

- Follow up.

- Follow up.

Get the message? Phone people who seemed willing to support your cause. Mail notices of your next meeting. Send details about a special fund-raising event. Make a sales call to potential customers. Whatever you do, *don't* let your prospects slip away.

SPORTS BANQUETS

Sports is education, the truest kind of education, that of character.

—RENÉ MAHEU

Organizing a sports banquet to celebrate a winning season? To honor a terrific coach? To acknowledge the most outstanding player?

Someone will have to say a few words to fit the occasion. If you're the person in charge, maybe you can talk about one of these topics:

The Importance of Teamwork

Red Holzman, the New York Knick coach, praised teamwork this way:

> On a good team there are no superstars. There are great players, who show they are great players by being able to play with others, as a team. They have the ability to be superstars, but if they fit into a good team, they make sacrifices, they do the things necessary to help the team win.

Share some insights into the special teamwork of your players.

The Value of Building Character

Player's agent Lewis Schaffel once said, "Talent is overrated. You win with character. In a short series, talent might prevail. Over an 82-game [basketball] season, character prevails."

Tell some real-life stories that show the fine character of your players.

A Witty Definition of Your Sport

For example, H. J. Dutiel defined baseball as "a game which consists of tapping a ball with a piece of wood, then running like a lunatic." Oliver Herford called fishing, "The art of taking more fish out of a stream than were ever in it."

You can use irreverent definitions as a springboard to discuss various aspects of your sport.

The Sheer Joy of the Game

Does the smell of a catcher's mitt bring back great memories? Does the sound of a tennis ball hitting the sweet spot seem like music to your ears? Does the sight of a 50-yard pass make you want to stand up and cheer? Share your joy of the game with the audience.

Red Smith expressed his joy of baseball this way: "Ninety feet between bases is perhaps as close as man has ever gotten to perfection."

The Benefits of Sports

Has a strong athletic league been a unifying force in your community? Has victory on the basketball court given your junior high kids something to cheer about? Has a charismatic coach inspired your students to try harder?

If you put athletic victories into *human* terms, your statistics will become even more impressive.

The Wide Appeal of Sports

Almost everybody likes sports. Why? Well, consider this reasoning by Earl Warren, chief justice of the Supreme Court:

> "I always turn to the sports section first. The sports section records people's accomplishments; the front page, nothing but a man's failures."

Previous Winners

Saluting this year's most valuable player? Cite some winners from previous years, and describe how they continue to pursue sports.

The Role of the Coach

What does *your* coach do that makes him special? What contributions has she made? How does he motivate and manage the team?

When Jackie Sherrill was athletic director at Texas A&M, he spoke to alumni groups about his role as head football coach:

> Coaching has changed. Twenty years ago, the coach never left the campus. Now I balance the budget, market the product, do promotions, handle personnel, sell the program, recruit, and coach. Like it or not, it's a different type of business now.

Some Humor

When Green Bay Packer lineman Henry Jordan shared a banquet dais with Vince Lombardi, he joked, "Seriously, coach Lombardi is very fair. He treats us all like dogs."

The Thrill of Winning

Committed to winning? Then remember Napoleon's advice: "If you start to take Vienna—take Vienna."

Al McGuire, who coached Marquette to the NCAA championship, made this comment:

> Once you start keeping score, winning's the bottom line. It's the American concept. If not, it's like playing your grandmother, and even then you try to win—unless she has a lot of money and you want to get some of it.

Pride in Your Accomplishments

When Joe Namath retired, he said the thing he was most proud of was "coming back from the adversity of those injuries. I never played as well as I would have liked to have played, but I played for 13 seasons when my doctor thought I would play for four. And I played despite a lot of adversity."

If you express genuine pride in your track record, the audience will sense your sincerity and share in your pride.

SUBSTITUTE SPEAKING

All is flux, nothing stays still.

—HERACLEITUS

You're sitting in your office, the phone rings, and it's your boss, asking you to pinch-hit as a last-minute substitute speaker.

Of course you agree, since it feels more like a summons than an invitation. Then panic hits. What can you possibly say, especially when the audience has been looking forward to hearing someone else?

Relax. You're not the first person to be squeezed into a substitute speaking slot. These guidelines should help.

Acknowledge You're a Substitute

The audience already knows you're just filling in, so you might as well be gracious about it. Say you're pleased to step in and speak to them. If you have trouble expressing this sentiment without gagging, rehearse it a few times in the privacy of your bedroom. Keep repeating it until you really *do* feel pleased to be the substitute speaker.

Don't Gripe About the Short Notice

I once heard a grim-faced substitute complain, "I was just asked to give this speech when I came to work today, so I'm not really sure what to say." Need I remind you that this is hardly a way to warm up an audience? Lighten up—and stop griping.

126

Try a Little Humor

Woody Allen has a great line: "Showing up is 80 percent of life." Maybe you can use this as an ice-breaker. After all, just showing up and being willing to give the speech means you're 80 percent successful!

Don't Worry About Being As Good As the Invited Speaker

Look at it this way: would anyone in the audience be willing to trade places and stand in *your* shoes at the lectern? No way. They're all relieved *you're* the one who has to give the speech. So don't worry about meeting the audience's standards. Take Dale Carnegie's advice: "If you are speaking, forget everything but the subject. Never mind what others are thinking of you or your delivery. Just forget yourself and go ahead."

Speak From Your Own Perspective

You're under no obligation to second-guess the original speaker. In fact, you're under no obligation to stick to the same topic. If you don't like the assigned title, change it. It's *your* lectern now, so you can tell your own story and call your own shots.

Above All, Follow Franklin Delano Roosevelt's Advice

FDR once said, "Be sincere; be brief, be seated." Substitute speakers can find no better advice.

TOASTS

May you live all the days of your life.

—OLD IRISH TOAST

When President Bush made a historic visit to Poland in 1989, he ad-libbed a toast—urging that country's factions to "rise above the mistrust, to bring the Polish people together for a common purpose."

Then he asked General Jaruzelski to make a toast. Apparently, the general was caught off guard by the President's impromptu request. When Bush saw the surprised look on the general's face, he quickly grabbed the General's arm and said, "You don't have to do it." But the Polish leader came through, managing to ad-lib a toast that brought applause from the guests.

I suppose there are a couple of lessons in this story: you never know when you'll be asked to give a toast, and there never really is a gracious way out of it.

No matter how surprised—and unprepared—you might feel, the best thing to do is *gather your wits and give the toast.*

Please: no stammering, no apologies, no gee-I-never-thought-I'd-have-to-give-a-toast disclaimers. Just make the toast.

Of course, maybe you'll be lucky. Maybe they'll ask you ahead of time, so you can prepare a good toast. These suggestions should give you some ideas.

Anniversary Toast

Throwing a party to salute 25 years of marriage? To celebrate the first year of a new business? To acknowledge 10 years of a successful partnership?

Make a toast not just to the years themselves, but to the good things they represent.

128

When my Aunt Ruth and Uncle Ab celebrated their golden wedding anniversary, another uncle, Bill Bailes, gave a wonderful toast that put their 50th anniversary into perspective:

> I would like to propose a toast to Ruth and Ab Houseknecht on the celebration of 50 years of marriage. Although a toast to that occasion should be enough, I do not think it would be complete. And so, Ruth and Ab, I would also like to toast:

- The countless hours of entertainment, good times and hospitality you've provided for your friends.

- Your endless devotion to your church.

- Your unselfish involvement in your community.

- Your unwavering support of your families.

- Your commitment to making this a better place for us all.

> May this occasion bring you many more years in good health! And now, ladies and gentlemen, would you please join me in a toast to Mr. and Mrs. Houseknecht, Ruth and Ab.

Upon receiving such a warm toast, my uncle Ab then stood up, thanked everyone for coming, and quipped he'd throw another big anniversary bash in another 50 years.

New-Baby Toast

- *Use an inspirational quotation.* Need a good source for inspirational lines? Check out a greeting card store. No kidding. Greeting cards are filled with short, touching, inspirational lines that can often double as terrific toasts.

- *Pay tribute to the parents.* And grandparents too!

- *Make a toast to the child's health and happiness.*

Birthday Toast

- *Express affection and gratitude.* Journalist Murray Teigh Bloom offered this toast to his wife on her 70th birthday: "Here's to Dellie, who's brought smiles or friendship or love to all of us here, and all of them to most of us."

- *Toast the person's health.*

- *Wish the person many more years of good times.* "May you live as long as you want, and never want as long as you live."

Wedding Toast

- *Define marriage.* Drink to "a taste of paradise"—Shalom Aleichem; "the best method for getting acquainted"—Heywood Broun; "an armed alliance against the outside world"—G. K. Chesterton.

- *Wish the bride and groom health, happiness, and prosperity.* Hard to go wrong with this triple blessing!

- *Wish them a smooth life.* A traditional toast to the bridal couple: "May all your troubles be little ones."

- *Wish all the celebrants much joy.* A toast straight from Shakespeare: "I drink to the general joy o' the whole table."

- *Toast both sets of parents.*

Three Final Cautions:

Beware of last-minute jitters. A salesman once told me about the time he thought he'd "wing" a toast at his son's wedding. By the time he finally stood up to offer the wedding toast, he'd already had a few stiff drinks. And out came "Here's to my son—and to his first wife." Ouch.

Pay attention to previous toasts, so you can respond accordingly. At the end of the Revolutionary War, Ben Franklin, as America's minister in Europe, attended a dinner in Paris with the British ambassador and the French 'foreign minister.

The British ambassador offered a toast "to George the Third, who, like the sun at noonday, spreads his light and illuminates the world." The French minister toasted "His Majesty, Louis the Sixteenth, who, like the moon, fills the earth with a soft, benevolent glow."
Franklin managed to top them both with this toast: "To George Washington, general of the armies of the United States, who, like Joshua of old, commanded both the sun and the moon to stand still, and both obeyed."

If you're worried about omitting someone, cover yourself by including *everyone*. This old toast might do the trick: "Here's to the whole world, lest some damn fool take offense."

WORDS OF WELCOME

Welcome is the best dish in the kitchen.

—OLD SCOTTISH SAYING

Want to greet new staff members? Say hello to a fresh group of volunteers? Welcome the freshman class to your school?

Offer a few words of welcome that will:

- make them feel at home

- recognize their special talents

- respect their various backgrounds

- get them in the right mood

- tell them about your organization

- let them know what's ahead

Here are some ideas that have worked for others:

Encourage New Members to Plunge Right In

When Joan Konner, dean of Columbia University Graduate School of Journalism, delivered opening day remarks to the class of 1990, she said:

> Everything you do, everyone you meet, every book you read, every event you attend will tell you a story, and possibly a truth. . . .

132

So keep your eyes open. Then let your mind go to work on what you see. Out will pop a reality of your own making.

If you report it accurately and responsibly, you'll be a fine reporter.

If you discern the pattern underlying it, you are a scientist.

And if you can make others see something new, or something old in a new way, you're an artist, discovering a reality and shaping it as well.

The best reporters are all of these.

And now it's time to get out of the taxi and to go out into the field. You've got the background. It's time to find the story.

Build a Theme Around the Motto of Your Organization

Does your school, group, or business have an official motto? You can build a theme around that slogan.

Cite Your Goals For the Coming Year

Do you plan to open *x* new stores? Increase test scores by *x* percent? Build a better image in the community? Now's the time to share your goals with the people who will help achieve them.

Talk About the Benefits

What's ahead for this new group? What can they look forward to? What rewards await them?

When Marion Ross, professor of economics at Mills College, addressed the students, she pointed out the benefits of a liberal arts education:

133

To play a musical instrument is to speak a universal language. To study dance is to acquire grace for a lifetime. To study philosophy is to ask the right questions and to learn that not all questions have answers. To read German literature is to meet Faust, whom you will meet again and again, and I trust, recognize.

Encourage a Sense of Teamwork

When you welcome your new members on board, make them feel part of the team right from the start. Talk about the standards of your group, so they know what's expected of them. Also talk about the resources of your group, so they know where they can turn for extra support.

Find Some Humor in the Situation

At the Washington swearing-in ceremony of U.S. Attorney General Nicholas Katzenbach and Deputy Attorney General Ramsey Clark, President Lyndon Johnson welcomed the two on board with this quip: "A town that can't support one lawyer can always support two." Hard to argue with that.

PART 2

LESSONS IN COURAGE

DO YOU FEEL A LITTLE NERVOUS?

Stage fright is the sweat of perfection.

—EDWARD R. MURROW

It was supposed to be a thrilling night. Sir John Gielgud, the British actor, had just completed his first production, *Romeo and Juliet*, with the Oxford University Dramatic Society. Unfortunately, all sorts of hitches had crept into the opening performance, and by the final curtain Gielgud was suffering from terrible nervous tension.

He had intended to step to the front of the stage and pay wonderful compliments to the show's leading ladies. Alas, all the fine tributes flew out of his head, and the only thing he could utter was a fumbled thank-you to "two leading ladies, the like of whom I hope I shall never meet again."

Chalk up another victory for the jitters!

The fact is, people get nervous when they have to give a speech. And, all sorts of amazing things come out of their mouths—including, at times, total silence.

When *Mister Roberts* was published, its author, Thomas Heggen, was asked to make some public appearances to promote the book. At his first speaking engagement, he was paralyzed with apprehension—unable to eat or enjoy himself at the luncheon.

Finally called upon to speak, he stood up—and not a word came out. Sheer, cruel silence.

Some kind person saw his agony and gently prodded him by saying, "Perhaps you can tell us how you wrote your book."

At this point, Heggen gulped and blurted out this contribution to the annals of public speaking history: "Well, s——, it was just that I was on this boat . . ."

Saying the wrong thing, going blank, uttering something totally obscene—ah, yes, these are just a few of the things that can go wrong when nervousness takes over.

137

And speakers suffer from less dramatic but equally troublesome problems: squeaky voices, dry mouths, trembling hands, sweaty palms, mysterious coughs—the list goes on and on.

The fact is, *most* people feel nervous when they have to say a few words, not just novices but even accomplished speakers.

The difference is that novices let their nervousness get the better of them, while accomplished speakers harness their nervousness to improve their performance.

You see, nervousness is just energy, plain and simple. Now, if you direct that energy, you can actually make it work to your advantage. You can turn it into a positive force that will enhance your delivery.

But if you allow your nervousness to go unchecked—if you allow *it* to control *you*—then you're going to be in trouble. Big trouble. Your nervousness will take over and plague you with a whole host of problems.

So the question isn't, "Gee, will I be nervous?" Everybody feels some nervous tension. "How can I turn my nervous energy into something positive?"— That's the real question. And yes, I can help you find some answers.

I can show you how to take your extra energy and channel it into strong eye contract, expressive body language, and vocal enthusiasm. These physical activities provide a good outlet for nervousness.

What's more, strong eye contract, expressive body language, and vocal enthusiasm will build your confidence. After all, it's hard to feel insecure when you look directly at your listeners and see the responsiveness in their faces.

PRE-SPEECH TRICKS TO PREVENT NERVOUSNESS

Every trade has its tricks, and public speaking is no exception. Here are some pre-speech tricks that professional speakers use to control nervousness:

Try Physical Exercise

Just before you give a speech, try to create some private time for yourself. I know this can be hard: when you're at the office, the phones ring; when you're at a luncheon, the guests clamor for your attention; when you're at a professional conference, the schedule can be grueling. It's hard to break away from the day's demands, but you've got to try. If necessary, escape to the bathroom and lock yourself in a stall. Even the pestiest of people will leave you alone at that point!

Once you've created some privacy, try some physical exercises. Concentrate on the part of your body that feels most tense. Your jaw? Your shoulders? Your hands? Deliberately tighten that part even more, until it starts to quiver. Then just let go. You'll feel an enormous sense of relief. Repeat a few times.

Drop your head. Let your cheek muscles go loose and your mouth go slack. Enjoy the easy feeling.

Make funny faces. Open your mouth and eyes wide, then close them tightly.

Stretch your arms in the air, slowly left, slowly right. Let that nervous energy go right out your fingertips. Keep your movements small and steady. You don't want to flail your arms wildly and work up a sweat, you just want to convert your nervous energy into controlled, relaxing movements.

Yawn a couple of times to loosen your jaw. This should feel good. Even more fun, pretend you're an opera singer. Try "mi, mi, mi," a few times. Go ahead—wave your arms as you do it.

Try Mental Exercises

Your mind can be a great ally. Reach into your grab bag of pleasant memories and pick one. Picture yourself floating down a country creek on a raft, swimming in a clear mountain lake, or walking on a quiet beach, feeling the sand between your toes. Draw these mental pictures to create your own private, pre-speech haven.

Or think of an influential person in your life, a mentor, perhaps, or a parent; anyone who would want you to do well. Take encouragement from that person.

When actress Glenn Close was offered an honorary degree from her alma mater, the College of William and Mary, she naturally felt flattered. But as she thought about actually giving the commencement address, she said her feet began to get "colder and colder."

How did Ms. Close tackle her emotions and manage to give a tremendously successful speech? She took inspiration from her mentor, as she relates in this excerpt:

> Who am I and what can I *say*? I was tempted many times to pick up the phone and tell President Verkuil that a speech was out of the question, but then I heard the voice of Howard Scammon, my friend and mentor. He was head of the theater department while I was here, and I saw him in my mind's eye standing in the wings at Phi Beta Kappa Hall in his strawberry Bermuda shorts and floppy sandals with his fists clenched, hissing in a stage whisper, *'Just go out there and do it!'* So . . . here I am.

Try a Rational Approach

Say to yourself, "I'm prepared. I've worked on this speech for three weeks. I'm ready." Or "I'm glad I can talk to this group. They really need to learn about my topic." Or "This is my specialty. I know this field inside and out."

Be logical. Be rational. List all of your advantages as a speaker. If you still need a boost, compare yourself favorably with other speakers. Tell yourself, "Well, I may not be a perfect speaker, but I'm sure a lot better than that boring 'expert' who showed upside-down slides and ran 10 minutes overtime." This is guaranteed to improve your confidence level!

Don't be embarrassed to look at the event as an opportunity to help *yourself*. Ask yourself, "What can *I* get out of this speech?" For example, "Giving this speech will make me more visible in the company." Or,

"I'll be able to meet some interesting people." Or, "This speech will help me get some new clients."

At this point, if you *still* feel a little scared to give your speech, try thinking of something that *really* terrifies you. Suddenly giving a speech should look pretty good, just by comparison.

For example, a young career woman told me she just keeps repeating, "This is better than death, this is better than death." And you know what? She's right. Giving a speech *is* better than death. And if that's how you've got to think about it, well, so be it.

Try Visualization

Athletes regularly use visualization to play better games. Jack Nicklaus once said, "I never hit a shot, not even in practice, without having a very sharp, in-focus picture of it in my head."

Relief pitcher Al Hrabosky said, "What I do is mentally picture myself pitching to a batter and striking him out."

Before Canadian figure skater Elizabeth Manley captured a silver medal at the Olympics, she imagined herself performing perfect triple lutzes. In her own mind, she ran through the sort of performance she'd need to impress the judges.

Athletes use visualization because they know it works; speakers can benefit by using these same techniques. Try a "test run" before your next speech. Visualize *exactly* what will happen after you're introduced. See yourself getting out of your chair, holding the speech in your hand, walking confidently across the stage, holding your head high, looking directly at the person who introduced you. Don't leave out any details. It's important to be as specific as possible. See *everything* from start to finish—including an enthusiastic round of applause from the audience.

If you see yourself as confident and successful in your mental test run, you'll feel confident and successful in your delivery.

TRICKS TO OVERCOME NERVOUSNESS
DURING THE SPEECH

All right, let's say you've followed my advice so far. You've prepared some good remarks. You've done some pre-speech exercises to keep your nerves in check. Now you're at the lectern, giving your speech, and everything seems to be okay, and—uh-oh, your mouth starts to go dry.

Time to panic? No. Just pause for a second and intensify your eye contact. If you concentrate on the audience instead of yourself, your nervousness should disappear.

By the way, don't worry about stopping for a moment. Audiences like it when speakers take a pause. Your moment of silence gives the audience a chance to collect its thoughts. Remember, listening is hard work too!

Still feel too dry to speak? Pause again, have a nice sip of water, enjoy the moment of peace, make good eye contact with the audience, and plunge in.

Remember this wonderful advice from Lady Bird Johnson: "The way you overcome shyness is to become so wrapped up in something else that you forget to be afraid." True, very true.

So, if any little problems pop up, take care of them—and move on with your speech. These tips should help you cope with any other mini traumas you might face at the podium:

Shaking Hands

Unless your audience is equipped with binoculars—and trust me, that's highly unlikely—they probably can't see your trembling hands. But if the shakes are distracting *you*, then you'd better do something about it. Move your body. Change the position of your feet. Lean forward to make a point. Gesture with your arms—no stingy little gesture, thank you; make it a really grand one.

A Pounding Heart

Unless your audience is equipped with stethoscopes—and again I promise, the chances are slim—they won't be able to hear your pounding heart. Really. Truly. *Just look at the audience*—and your self-consciousness will disappear.

A Quivery Voice

Again, the secret is intensify your eye contact. Focus on *them*. Pause for a moment as you look out there. Then pitch your voice lower and control your breath as you begin to speak. Speak slowly. Really wrap yourself around those words.

Take heart from Abraham Lincoln. When he gave the Gettysburg Address, he was visibly nervous at the beginning, his voice shrill and his movements awkward. But after his initial discomfort wore off, his speech took on a life of its own.

A Tickle in Your Throat

If you have to cough, cough—away from the microphone, please. Do it and get it over with. Drink some water before you continue, or pop a piece of cough drop into your mouth, if necessary. I always keep a cough drop handy when I speak, unwrapped, so I don't have to fumble with papers in front of audience, and broken into small pieces so I don't have to stand there trying to talk with a huge lozenge bulging in my cheek. And you know what? I've never once had to use that cough drop! I think there's a perverse law of nature: if you need a cough drop, you won't have one handy; if you have one, you won't need it.

So arm yourself with a cough drop. Think of it as a bizarre form of "podium insurance," something whose mere presence will prevent a coughing fit.

A Sweaty Forehead

Auditoriums can get hot, and nervousness can make them feel even hotter. If you start to sweat, wipe it away with a big cotton handkerchief that you've also placed at the lectern. Don't hesitate to really *wipe*. No sense in making discreet dabs—they're ineffectual, and you'll have to dab repeatedly. Besides, there's no such thing as a "discreet" dab when you're standing in front of an audience; they see a little dab as well as a big wipe, so you might as well give them their money's worth. Wipe well the first time, and get it over with.

Runny Nose and Watery Eyes

Bright lights can trigger these responses. Just pause, say "Excuse me," blow your nose, wipe your eyes, and get on with your speech. No big deal, no big apologies. A simple "excuse me" is all you have to say.

May I be graphic for a moment? I have seen some speakers blow their nose at the lectern and then—yes, yes, it's true—actually look down at the junk in their handkerchief. I know *you* wouldn't do a thing like that. But if you ever witness such a spectacle, would you please send the speaker a copy of this book and highlight this section? Send it anonymously, if you wish, but send it. You'll be doing everyone a favor—alerting a speaker who's unaware of this disgusting habit, and sparing audiences any future demonstrations.

Burping

When some people get nervous, they feel they have to burp. If that's the case with you, be extra faithful about doing relaxation exercises before you speak. And use some common sense: don't drink any carbonated beverages before your speech, and don't eat anything heavy. If you must eat, choose easily digestible foods and eat them slowly. Don't gulp. And don't talk while you eat.

Fumbled Words

Professional speakers trip over words all the time. Don't believe me? Watch network news for a week and count the number of misspoken words that come out of the anchors' mouths. This should make you feel better. After all, if some guy getting a million dollars a year is allowed to fumble words in front of millions of viewers, surely the world won't crumble if you trip on a phrase at your monthly managers' meeting.

If you make a minor fumble, just keep going.

If you make a major fumble, just stop, correct yourself, smile to show you're human, and continue.

Make an effort to slow down a bit. Fumbles tend to come in bunches. Why? Because a fumble is often a symptom that you're concentrating too much on yourself and not on your message. Take it as a warning to slow down and focus on your thoughts. Don't make elaborate apologies. It isn't worth it. Just plow on.

Fumbled Objects

Note cards fall on the floor? Pointer flies out of your hand? An important exhibit slides off the table? Take heart. It's happened before to other poor souls, and they survived.

At his Viennese debut, cellist Pablo Casals suffered from a case of nervousness. When he picked up his bow to play the first note, he found that his hand was too tense. To relax his hand, he tried a little twirl. Alas, his bow flew from his fingers and landed smack in the middle of the orchestra. As he sat there, watching the rows of musicians pass it back to him, he remembered his mother's advice about staying calm. And by the time his bow was returned to him, his hand was steady—and he was ready to perform an outstanding concert.

145

THE SURVIVAL KIT FOR SPEAKERS

Whenever you have to give a speech, double-check to make sure you've got:

_____ *A glass of water.* Already poured, with no ice, so it's ready to drink. When you're suffering from a case of dry mouth or you're in the middle of a coughing fit, you don't need the extra hassle of pouring a glass of water in front of a peering audience. I once saw a speaker get so nervous that she spilled the whole pitcher, soaking both her notes and her suit.

_____ *A handkerchief.* Clean, white, and cotton. No paper tissues, please. They can stick to a sweaty face and leave a speaker looking pretty foolish.

_____ *A cough drop.* Unwrapped and broken into small bits, ready to pop into your mouth.

HOW TO HANDLE DIFFICULT, EMOTIONAL MOMENTS

It's a familiar response: You're giving the eulogy at a funeral service, or making a farewell speech at your retirement dinner, or saying good-bye to someone who's resigned from your firm.

And—oh no—you start to choke up. What should you do? Fight back your tears? Give up and let them flow? Continue speaking as best you can? Or stop talking and walk away—fast—before you break down and cry in front of all those people?

It's a difficult moment. As a person, you're feeling sad. And yet in your role as a public speaker, you feel obligated to keep your emotions in check.

146

Of course, even happy moments can be emotionally difficult. Maybe you're accepting a tribute from your church, or getting honored by a civic organization, or being surprised with a terrific birthday party. All happy moments, yes, but happy moments can trigger tears too.

When country music star Conway Twitty accepted the Living Legend Award for more than 25 years of musical achievement, he was touched by the standing ovation—and broke into tears. In his acceptance speech, he introduced his mother in the audience and said, "See, Mama. I told you not to worry."

How would *you* respond to an emotional situation? It's hard to predict. After all, emotions are funny things.

But if you plan to give a speech at an emotional event—a funeral, a retirement, a wedding, whatever—it might be smart to think *now* about the way you might handle your emotions.

Maybe you *won't* be bothered by tears. When Anjelica Huston accepted an Academy Award, she saw her father crying and she saw her friend Jack Nicholson crying, yet she somehow stayed "dry as a bone."

But, just in case *you* don't stay so dry, maybe these real-life stories will prove inspirational and instructional:

- When President Bush paid tribute to the 47 dead crew members of the battleship *Iowa*, he said, "They came from Hidalgo, Texas, and Cleveland, Ohio; from Tampa, Florida and Costa Mesa, California. They came to the Navy as strangers, served the Navy as shipmates and friends, and left the Navy as brothers in eternity."

  An audience of 3,000 grief-stricken people listened as the president's words soon gave way to emotion. His voice cracked as he said, "Your men are under a different command now, one that knows no rank, only love; knows no danger, only peace." And, at this point, tears filled President Bush's eyes.

  Apparently, the president feared he would lose control, so he dropped the final lines of his address, managed to say, "May God bless them," swallowed hard, turned abruptly, and left the lectern.

  After his speech, the President and Mrs. Bush walked among the aisles of mourners, comforting them and embracing them. During difficult moments, Mrs. Bush wept openly. President Bush managed to keep his tears in check—but was smart enough to keep a handkerchief clutched in his hand, just in case.

• Robert Pelka, a sixth-grade teacher at PS 94 in New York City, received an engraved plaque from his graduating students honoring him as "the Most Outstanding Teacher." He also received a leather album filled with sentimental letters from each student. The emotion of it all touched Mr. Pelka. He said, "These children would have made it with any teacher. I've never been so honored in my life." And then, he wasn't able to say any more—so he just stopped speaking.

• When survivors of the ill-fated battle of Gallipoli gathered for a 75th anniversary, the emotion of the day was almost too much to bear. During one of the memorials for Britain's dead, 94-year-old veteran Jimmy Page kissed Prime Minister Margaret Thatcher's hand and said, "Please forgive me for crying, but the occasion is too much for me."

He need not have felt alone. While a stiff upper lip is a time-honored military tradition, history books tell us that there are plenty of living legends who were not ashamed to shed tears.

• When General Lee bade farewell to his troops, he rode slowly along the lines of soldiers—with tears flowing freely down his cheeks.

• On Christmas Eve, at midnight mass at St. Patrick's Cathedral, Mayor Ed Koch received an emotional public farewell from John Cardinal O'Connor.
    The Cardinal said, "It would be difficult to imagine a mayor of New York who has been more supportive of the church than has been Mayor Koch." When the huge congregation broke into sustained applause, the mayor seemed to fight back his tears.
    The Cardinal smiled and broke the tension by saying, "If every one of those people had voted, you'd still be mayor."

- When singer Kathleen Ferrier was rehearsing Mahler's "Song of the Earth" with Bruno Walter, the beauty of the words and the music simply overwhelmed her. She couldn't continue, and they had to take a break in their rehearsal.

  She apologized to Bruno Walter, but he replied, "Kathleen, you have nothing to be sorry about. You see, we all should have been weeping."

Indeed.

PART 3

LESSONS IN STYLE AND DELIVERY

HOW TO ADD SPARKLE TO ANY SPEECH

Some speeches linger in the hearts and minds of audiences. Other speeches are forgotten as soon as the speaker walks away from the podium.

What makes a speech memorable? Style.

Here are some professional speechwriting devices that will add style to *your* speeches:

ANECDOTES

Remember when you were a kid and you loved listening to stories? Well, there's still a little bit of this kid in all of us. Even the most sophisticated audiences like to hear good anecdotes. Give them what they want.

- Jesse Jackson shared this personal story to create a theme for his speech to the Democratic Convention:

America is not a blanket, woven from one thread, one color, one cloth. When I was a child in South Carolina, and Momma couldn't afford a blanket, she didn't complain and we didn't freeze. Instead, she took pieces of old cloth—patches—wool, silk, gaberdeen, crockersack—only patches, barely good enough to shine your shoes with. But they didn't stay that way long. With sturdy hands and strong cord, she sewed them together into a quilt, a thing of power, beauty, and culture. Now we must build a quilt together.

- When President Bush addressed the United Nations General Assembly, he shared this anecdote:

> I was the permanent representative of the United States. I was 45 minutes late going to the meeting [of the U.N. Security Council]. And all 45 minutes were filled by the first speaker to take the floor. And when I walked in and took my seat, the speaker paused with great courtesy and said as follows: "I welcome the permanent representative of the United States and now, for his benefit, I will start my speech all over again from the beginning."
> That's a true story. And at that moment, differences of alliance, ideology, didn't matter. The universal groan that went up around that table from every member present, and then the laughter that followed, united us all.

COLLOQUIAL LANGUAGE

Slang, colorful expressions, regional sayings; they all add sparkle to a speech.

- When Senator Bill Bradley played basketball on an episode of *The Cosby Show*, he noted it was only the third time he's played ball since retiring from the Knicks in 1977. Why? "While my heart is in it, my knees ain't."

- In a speech in Peoria, Illinois, President Eisenhower used everyday language to appeal to his audience: "Farming looks mighty easy when your plow is a pencil, and you're a thousand miles from a cornfield."

DEFINITIONS

Ever notice how often speakers say, "According to Webster . . ." and then bore the audience with long, technical definitions that they lifted straight from the dictionary?

If you want to define something, come up with an *interesting* definition.

- Franklin Delano Roosevelt offered these clever definitions in a radio speech:

  A radical is a man with both feet planted firmly in the air. A conservative is a man with two perfectly good legs, who, however, has never learned to walk. A reactionary is a somnambulist walking backward.

- In his inaugural speech, New Jersey Governor James Florio defined *security* in terms that New Jersians could relate to:

  Security. That's another ideal. It means a lot of things. It means going to the shore, knowing that you can enjoy its majesty, its beauty, its power without worrying about needles and garbage. . . .
  Security also means freedom from drugs. A safe, secure childhood is a cherished ideal we share.

LISTS

Need to make a number of points and want to present them in an organized, easy-to-follow manner? Try listing your points.

When Dr. Mitsuru Misawa, president of the Industrial Bank of Japan Leasing, spoke to the seventh Japan-Louisiana Conference, he used this list technique to good advantage:

Japanese direct investment, especially in U.S. real estate, has recently generated some negative reactions, or at least a sense of wary unease. I think there are several types of noticeable reactions.

First, some Americans fear that the Japanese, through massive investment, might gain leverage to influence the national economy and government of the United States.

Second, more specifically, many Americans are afraid that strategically sensitive skills and technologies, vital for national defense, might be controlled by the Japanese.

Third, foreign direct investment in many cases places vital managerial decisions in the hands of foreign business executives, raising the specter of total divestiture, factory closings, and worker layoffs.

Fourth, in the eyes of the average American, Japanese management methods are something alien to American culture.

Fifth, Japanese expatriates and their families tend to form a separate enclave and stand aloof from the local community.

After listing these emotional fears, Dr. Misawa then responded with sound, logical reasoning to refute these negative feelings.

PARALLEL STRUCTURE

Use parallel structure to provide a sense of balance and create the emotional appeal of harmony.

A classic example of parallel structure—this prayer of Saint Francis of Assisi:

Lord, make me an instrument of your peace. Where there is hatred, let me sow love; where there is injury, pardon; where there is discord, union; where there is doubt, faith; where there is despair, hope; where there is darkness, light; and where there is sadness, joy.

156

Some uses of parallel structure in the political world:

- President Eisenhower: "Every gun that is made, every warship launched, every rocket fired, signifies, in the final sense, a theft from those who hunger and are not fed, those who are cold and are not clothed."

- President Johnson: "Aggression unchallenged is aggression unleashed."

- President Ford: "When I talk about energy, I am talking about jobs. . . . No energy, no jobs."

- President Kennedy: "If a free society cannot help the many who are poor, it cannot save the few who are rich."

PERSONAL DETAILS

By sharing some of your personal history with the audience, you will create an emotional bond and build a strong rapport.

When T. Marshall Hahn, Jr., chairman and CEO of Georgia-Pacific Corporation, gave a commencement speech at the University of Kentucky, he shared this delightful bit of personal history with the audience:

It is a particular pleasure to be home and to participate in yet another University of Kentucky commencement. I attended my first commencement here some 63 years ago, although unknowingly, since my mother graduated from the university in May, and I was born the following December.

I continued to accompany my mother to U of K commencements in the years that followed, when my father was a faculty member here and when funds for baby-sitters were scarce.

Of course, I attended my own graduation in 1945 . . . and came home for more of them when I returned to the university as

157

a faculty member after completing my graduate studies following World War II.

REPETITION

Repetition is crucial. Why? Because audiences get restless. Their minds wander. All sorts of distractions pop into their heads—deadlines, bills, kids, you name it. And whole sections of a speech often pass right by their ears.

So if you have a particularly good phrase, slogan, or line, use it. Again. And again.

If the audience missed it the first time, maybe they'll catch it the second time. Or the third.

Besides, even if the audience caught your message the first time, they'll appreciate hearing it again. Good lines are hard to come by. Audiences are more than happy to hear them repeated.

- James Meenaghan, CEO of the Home Insurance Company, before the Free Enterprise Award luncheon: "A Washington journalist named Ben Wattenberg has written that in American history, it is the optimists who have always turned out to be the realists. Let me repeat that: In American history, it is the optimists who have always turned out to be the realists."

- The Reverend Jesse Jackson: "We must give peace a chance. We must give peace a chance. We must, we must!

- Franklin Delano Roosevelt: "We must act, and we must act quickly."

- President Johnson: "There is no Negro problem. There is no Southern problem. There is no Northern problem. There is only an American problem."

158

- President Reagan, in his address to the 1988 Republican convention:

  Before we came to Washington, America had just suffered the two worst back-to-back years of inflation in 60 years. Those are the facts. And as John Adams said, "Facts are stubborn things."
  Interest rates had jumped to over 21 percent . . .
  Facts are stubborn things.
  Industrial production was down . . .
  Facts are stubborn things.
  . . . Fuel costs jumped through the atmosphere, more than doubling. Then people waited in gas lines as well as unemployment lines.
  Facts are stubborn things.

RHETORICAL QUESTIONS

Want to involve your audience? Rhetorical questions are a powerful technique. They encourage the audience to think about your topic and take a personal stand.

A tip: whenever you pose a rhetorical question, be sure to pause afterward, allowing the listeners some quiet time to answer the question in their own minds.

- When President Eisenhower heard the large budget that the Department of Defense requested, he asked, "How many times do we have to destroy Russia?"

- When House Speaker Jim Wright announced his resignation to the House of Representatives, he asked:

Have I been too partisan? Too insistent? Too abrasive? Too determined to have my way? Perhaps. Maybe so. If I've offended anybody in the other party, I'm sorry. I never meant to. . . .

Are there things I'd do differently if I had them to do over again? Oh, boy! How many may I name for you!

QUOTATIONS

Next to the originator of a good sentence is the first quoter of it.

—EMERSON

Audiences *love* quotations—if you:

Keep the Quotation Short and Snappy

Remember: A speech is meant to be *heard,* not read. The shorter and simpler your quotations, the easier for the audience to hear them and remember them.

Cut or paraphrase any "slow parts." Audiences want short, lively quotations that will stick in their minds.

Blend Your Quotation Into the Speech

Too many speakers just "sprinkle" quotations throughout their speech. Don't do this. If you "smooth" a quotation into your text, you will create a stronger emotional appeal.

When Lyndon Johnson gave a State of the Union address, he blended a Thomas Jefferson quotation into the theme of his speech: "Thomas Jefferson said no nation can be both ignorant and free. Today, no nation can be both ignorant and great."

Appear Comfortable With the Quotation

Make sure you can pronounce the source's name. Pity the poor speaker who quoted "the famous German writer, Goethe"—then mispronounced the writer's name to rhyme with "growth."

And pity the poor speaker who quoted one of his "favorite French writers, Albert Camus"—and mispronounced the name to sound like "cammus."

Such slipups do not inspire confidence in an audience.

STATISTICS

Some people think statistics are boring. These people haven't heard the right statistics. Statistics can add tremendous life and power and spunk to any speech—*if* you follow a few guidelines:

Put Statistics in Simple Terms

Don't just say, "The senator mails x million items to his constituents each year." Most listeners can't comprehend large numbers. Instead, put your statistics in simple, everyday terms: "This means the Senator sends five pieces of mail to each address in his district." Everyone with a mailbox can relate to that simple statistic.

Make Statistics Seem Real to Your Audience

When Dr. Karen Harlan spoke to women's groups about health-care issues, she knew how to make medical statistics seem real to her audience: "The chances of getting breast cancer are one in eleven. That means that of the twenty-two of us here, two will get breast cancer."

161

Round Off the Numbers

Don't say "997,499 customers." Say "almost a million customers." Remember: Your audience is *listening,* not reading. Their ears get only one chance to interpret your message. Make it easy for them to hear your statistics.

Create a Sense of Immediacy

Try something like: "While we're sitting here for an hour and debating the merits of sex education in our schools, *x* teenage girls will give birth to illegitimate children. We can't afford to just sit around and talk anymore; we need to act."

Be Graphic

When Senator Robert Byrd of West Virginia learned that America's trade deficit might drop to "only" $130 billion, he said this would be "like finding that your town is still going to be hit by Hurricane Gilbert, but that the winds have dropped to 'only' 150 miles an hour."

Use Numbers Sparingly

Audiences simply cannot comprehend more than a few statistics at a time. Don't overload their minds.

Don't Apologize For Using Statistics

I once heard a speaker apologize for "boring you with all these numbers." If she had followed the guidelines I've outlined here, her statistics wouldn't have been boring at all.

TRIADS

The human mind is strongly attracted to things that come in units of three.

From "Goldilocks and the Three Bears" to "Three strikes and you're out", from the three parts of the scientific method to the three parts of the Holy Trinity, humans are lulled and intrigued and comforted by triads. Abraham Lincoln knew what he was doing when he said, "We cannot dedicate, we cannot consecrate, we cannot hallow this ground."

Consider these contemporary examples:

- In his inaugural address, Jimmy Carter used this triad: "You have given me a great responsibility: to stay close to you, to be worthy of you, and to exemplify what you are."

- Manfred Wörner, secretary general of the North Atlantic Treaty Organization, quipped that the success of NATO used to be measured on three counts: "Keeping the Soviets out, keeping the Americans in, and keeping the Germans down."

PLAYING WITH THE SOUNDS OF WORDS

Rhyme, alliteration, word games, they can all add style. But an important caution: be careful you don't overdo it. A little rhyme is catchy; too much sounds like bad poetry.

Here are some good examples of wordplay:

- "Too often politicians play show-and-tell with education's needs before an election and then play hide-and-seek with those needs after an election." National Education Association president Mary Hatwood Futrell.

- "Drinking plus driving spell death and disaster." President Reagan.

- "When some of our students actually have trouble locating America on a map of the world, it is time for us to map a new approach to education." President Bush.

- "Ethics has no bottom line. It is not a commodity. We must always be mindful that our forefathers founded a land of opportunity, not of opportunists." Brown University president Vartan Gregorian.

- "The people who support a woman's right to chose abortion have reproduced. The feminist fringe has become the feminist family." Actress Marlo Thomas.

SHORT SENTENCES

Short sentences pack big power. They're easy for you to deliver, and easy for the audience to grasp.

When I teach speechwriting workshops at corporations, I ask the participants to analyze one of their typical speeches and to count the number of words in their sentences. When they start hitting 25, 35, 45 words per sentence, I show them how to cut away the fat. Audiences simply cannot follow long sentences.

Notice what short sentences Lyndon Johnson used when he spoke at the dedication of an airport in Morgantown, West Virginia: "Hunger destroys initiative. Ignorance destroys initiative. A cold and indifferent government destroys initiative."

164

The average number of words in this section of Johnson's speech? Just over four words per sentence.

TITLES

Give your speech a title? Absolutely. Choosing a good title will help you focus your speech. Even more important, it will help the audience grasp your main message and remember your main point.

Make your title work for you. If possible, tie your title into the name of your business, the motto of your school, or the sales slogan of your company.

For example, as the author of *How to Write & Give A Speech* (New York: St. Martin's Press, 1984), I'm often asked to lecture on public speaking. I've developed one of my lectures into a marketing tool by giving it this title: "How to Write & Give a Speech—& Survive." Every time audiences hear this title, they're reminded of both my book and my speechwriting business.

Some ideas for clever titles? Use popular songs, movies, or best sellers as springboards. For example:

- "Libel and Newspapers: Is This the Big Chill?" Katharine Darrow; *The New York Times* Company.

- "Back to the Future Information Services: Or, Stuck in the Middle Again?" Patricia Diaz; Federal Communications Commission.

- "Go, Oh Thoughts, on Wings of Gold" Marion Ross, Professor of Economics at Mills College, inspired by an aria in Verdi's opera *Nabucco*.

Be irreverent, if you want. Be flip. Be daring. Just, please, don't be boring.

If your title sounds something like, "General Remarks on the State of the Company Upon Its Completion of 25 Challenging Years of Service," don't be too surprised if people's eyes glaze over. Scrap a boring title, and come up with something that *will* catch listeners' attention.

Once you come up with a good title, work it into the theme of your speech. When Benjamin Everidge, president of the Astronauts Memorial Foundation, spoke at the cornerstone dedication of that memorial, he gave his speech this title: "Honoring Those Who Brought the Stars a Little Closer." Then he created a strong emotional appeal by weaving this title into his opening:

> On a January morning three and a half years ago, the sudden loss of seven courageous astronauts aboard the space shuttle *Challenger* stunned and saddened the world.
>
> But out of that sadness grew a powerful determination that these seven, and the seven astronauts who had gone before them, would not have died in vain. That we would continue their life's devotion—to bring the stars a little closer.

VISUAL IMAGERY

Who can forget the "iron curtain" of Winston Churchill? Or the "big stick" of Teddy Roosevelt? Speeches that draw mental pictures create a special appeal for audiences:

- "We must especially be aware of that small group of selfish men who would clip the wings of the American eagle in order to feather their own nests." President Franklin Delano Roosevelt.

- "Wars are different from baseball games, where, at the end of the game, the teams get dressed and leave the park." President Truman.

166

- "You don't just redistribute bread, you create more bakeries." Jack Kemp, Secretary of Housing and Urban Development.

- "Reagan promised them a seven-course dinner. What they got was a possum and a six pack." Agriculture Commissioner Jim Hightower of Texas.

PART 4

RESOURCES

Resource Appendix: Where to Find Great Quotes and Anecdotes
Some Recommendations from the Author's Personal Library

ANECDOTES

Fadiman, Clifton, ed. *The Little, Brown Book of Anecdotes*. New York: Little, Brown, 1985. $29.95. I can't praise this book enough. You'll find more than 4,000 well-researched anecdotes about 2,000 famous people—from Hank Aaron to J. P. Morgan to Dylan Thomas. Keep a copy near your desk; you'll use it often. It offers an index of subjects, an index of names, a source list, and a bibliography. Great for browsing, too!

Hay, Peter, ed. *The Book of Business Anecdotes*. New York: Facts on File, 1988. $22.95. Conveniently organized by subject, from money, to selling, to corporate culture. Includes good stories about Carl Icahn's negotiating talents, John Wanamaker's mastery of advertising, T. S. Eliot's experience as a bank clerk, and more.

Morris, Desmond. *The Book of Ages*. New York: Penguin, 1983. $8.95. If you want to say a few words at someone's birthday party, turn to this book and find out who did what when. You'll find all sorts of anecdotes, trivia, and quotations for birthday celebrants of all ages, from newborn babies to folks topping 100:

- Age 52: Lady Astor quipped, "I refuse to admit that I'm more than 52, even if that does make my sons illegitimate."

- Age 60: Actor Herbert Beerbohm Tree: "I was born old and get younger every day. At present I am 60 years young."

Van Ekeren, Glenn, ed. *The Speaker's Sourcebook*. Englewood Cliffs, New Jersey: Prentice Hall, 1988. $14.95. A wide range of anecdotes, many of them inspirational and motivational. You'll find John D. Rockefeller on success, Rodney Dangerfield on marriage, Casey Stengel on leadership, Ted Turner on self-confidence, Woodrow Wilson on goals, and more. No index, no source list.

DEFINITIONS

Brussell, Eugene E, ed. *Webster's New World Dictionary of Quotable Definitions*. Englewood Cliffs, New Jersey: Prentice Hall, 1988. $29.95. Want a clever definition? Forget your regular dictionary. Turn to this book for more than 17,000 memorable definitions and one-liners on 2,000 subjects. A few samples:

> Banker: "A fellow who hands you his umbrella when the sun is shining and wants it back the minute it begins to rain." Mark Twain.
> Public Opinion: "What people think that other people think." Alfred Austin.

HUMOR

Perret, Gene, and Linda Perret, eds. *Funny Business*. Englewood Cliffs, NJ: Prentice Hall, 1990. $12.95. Filled with funny one-liners on virtually every aspect of business, including:

> Mandatory Retirement: "The company doesn't want you when you're old and useless. They prefer people who are young and useless."
> Productivity: "Productivity is the bottom line in business. If you're not producing, you'd better be related to the boss or one of his children."
> Long Lunches: "Some people take so long for lunch they could lose their seniority."
> Sign in Legal Department: THE BUCK STALLS HERE.

172

POLITICAL STORIES AND QUOTATIONS

Henning, Charles. *The Wit & Wisdom of Politics*. Golden, Colorado: Fulcrum, 1989. $12.95. Where else could you find:

- Mario Cuomo: "You campaign in poetry, you govern in prose."

- Adlai Stevenson: "A hypocrite is the kind of politician who would cut down a redwood tree, then mount the stump and make a speech for conservation."

- John Nance Garner: "Hell, don't tell me what the bill says. Tell me what it does."

- Jerry Brown: "Too often I find that the volume of paper expands to fill the available briefcases."

- Golda Meir: "Whether women are better than men I cannot say—but I can say they are certainly no worse."

Tomlinson, Gerald, ed. *Speaker's Treasury of Political Stories, Anecdotes & Humor*. Englewood Cliffs, New Jersey: Prentice Hall, 1990. $12.95. You'll find such quotes as:

- Andrew Jackson: "One man with courage makes a majority."

- Anatole France: "His instinct told him that it was better to understand a little than to misunderstand a lot."

As well as anecdotes:

A friend of Cato the Elder felt that Rome should have a statue honoring the great soldier. But Cato said, "No. I would rather have people ask why there is no statue to Cato than to ask why there is one."

Perhaps the most useful feature of the book is a calendar of political events. If you're giving a speech on June 3, for example, you can turn to this calendar and learn what happened in politics on June 3.

173

PROVERBS AND APHORISMS

Auden, W. H., and Louis Kronenberger, eds. *The Viking Book of Aphorisms*. New York: Penguin Books, 1966. $6.95. Where else could you find this gem by Goethe: "Know thyself? If I knew myself, I'd run away." Or this useful reminder by none other than Saint Thomas Aquinas: "Not everything that is more difficult is more meritorious." More than 3,000 wise and pithy comments.

Fergusson, Rosalind. *The Penguin Dictionary of Proverbs*. New York: Penguin Books, 1983. $5.95. Handy proverbs, easy-to-use chapters.

QUOTATIONS

Bartlett, John. *Bartlett's Familiar Quotations*. Boston: Little, Brown, 1980. $22.95. An important reference work, with more than 22,500 quotations. Especially strong in the Bible, the classics, and Shakespeare. Revised and updated to include contemporary figures such as Muhammad Ali and Mick Jagger. Outstanding index.

Bettmann, Otto L. *The Delights of Reading*. Boston: Godine, 1987. $14.95. If you love words, and the people who write, edit, read, and publish them, you'll love this book.

Camp, Wesley D., ed. *What a Piece of Work Is Man!* Englewood Cliffs, New Jersey: Prentice Hall, 1990. $12.95. An outstanding collection of unfamiliar quotations covering 4,000 years of human experience. Well organized, well documented. Topics include:

> Argument: "He who strikes the first blow admits he's lost the argument." Chinese proverb.
> Divorce: "Divorce is the psychological equivalent of a triple coronary bypass." Mary K. Blakely.
> Health: "If you wish to keep as well as possible, the less you think about your health, the better." Oliver Wendell Holmes.
> Loss: "You must lose a fly to catch a trout." George Herbert.
> Schools: "High school is closer to the core of the American experience than anything else I can think of." Kurt Vonnegut.